CRYPTOTRADING

PRO

Trade for a living with time-tested strategies, tools and risk management techniques. A contemporary guide from the beginner to the pro

Alan T. Norman

BONUS BOOK

Cryptocurrency Market Manipulations and How I Found Satoshi Nakamoto

Get the link in the end of the book

TABLE OF CONTENTS

PREFACE

In the era of the complete penetration of the Internet into every sphere of our lives, there are growing plurality of people no longer agree to white collar work in the office from nine to six. The new generation is unwilling to follow the beaten track of their grandfathers and great-grandfathers, who graduated from universities, chose a job and worked there till they reached retirement age. Furthermore, we are tired of constant deadlines at work, bosses with their eternally changeable moods and, most insulting, the lack of career and financial growth.

The Internet gave people an opportunity to break this vicious circle. People got an alternative that may provide both financial rewards and freedom from office work, senior managers and timeframes.

So, what is this fabulous alternative that gives the longed-for freedom to manage your own time and even the whole your life?

Most people dream of doing nothing (or almost nothing) and being paid for it, don't they? What if I told you this dream has almost become a reality?

One way or another, the Internet has provided humanity with a variety of options for passive earnings. While sitting on your couch, you can sell something, keep accounting records for someone, make posts for your blog or live on investment interest. Therefore, nowadays, you have every chance to have a good income in the future by investing even a small fraction of your abilities, time and capital in "passive" business, where there are no offices and bosses!

Previously, people earned passive income from investing in bank deposits, credit unions, various funds, and real estate. However, those dividends came slowly or with much work.

Now there are new "professions" for receiving passive income, including trading. No matter how difficult it may seem at first glance, almost anyone can master this "science". However, for the last decade, hundreds of thousands of traders around the world have devoted themselves to work on a variety of stock exchanges, striving to become millionaires. They sit in front of computers 24/7, storming exchanges and trying to increase their capital. Unfortunately, not everyone succeeds.

With the cryptocurrency burst into existence several years ago, a completely new subspecies of traders – crypto traders – appeared in the market. By and large, cryptocurrency trading does not differ much from typical trading The basic principle is the same: "Buy low, sell high." Regardless what product you have – stocks, oil, gold or cryptocurrency – this principle remains unchanged.

So, who are these "mysterious" crypto traders and what do you personally need to master this profession? To be successful in cryptocurrency trading as well as trading other assets, you will need:

- Free time
- Capital
- Basic awareness of economic concepts

- Desire to constantly learn and try new strategies;
- Mental stability

Although conventional trading and cryptocurrency trading have much in common, they still have their differences. Let's sort them out.

If you are an ordinary trader (NOT a cryptocurrency trader), then you know for sure that trading on your exchanges can be accessed only through a broker. A broker provides software for interaction with the exchange and provides technical support for such work. These services come at a price, but you have no choice since you cannot do without a broker on the stock exchange. However, if you trade cryptocurrency, you have access to any exchange. No matter your age, social status, profession or size of capital, you can fill out a registration form on an exchange's website (you'd better do it on several exchanges), deposit funds for trading and start your own path of a cryptocurrency trader without help from bystanders.

You should remember that the cryptocurrency market operates 24/7. It doesn't close nor open at a certain time like ordinary stock markets. That is, any cryptocurrency exchange is "alive" and works without sleep and rest.

One of the main advantages and challenges of cryptocurrency trading is volatility[1]. This indicator shows the range of fluctuations in the value of an asset for a certain period of time. It can be called

---

[1] In finance, volatility (symbol σ) is the degree of variation of a trading price series over time as measured by the standard deviation of logarithmic returns.

a prerequisite for trading since a trader profit from the difference between the purchase price and the sale price of an asset.

However, keep in mind that volatility is not a constant value. It depends on many factors and cannot be forecasted precisely (sometimes volatility is even created artificially to drive up the price for a particular currency). Traders make calculations on historical data, which has been formed in difficult market conditions and which will never repeat again. Therefore, it is worth treating indicators as an approximate benchmark.

But it is volatility which makes cryptocurrency so attractive for trading. Historical data has not yet accumulated (as cryptocurrency appeared only a few years ago and professional cryptocurrency trading is even younger), and complex market conditions happen right in front of your eyes.

Here I want to warn you that volatility can play into the hands of a successful trader, but it can also play dirty tricks on a newcomer.

Let's sum up the main pros and arguments in favor of cryptocurrency trading:

- Access to exchanges without the involvement of brokers
- Exchanges work 24/7
- Volatility

I think you have realized that cryptocurrency trading is not only a trendy passive income idea that requires pressing "start" and "stop" buttons. It's a constant generation of ideas and new strategies that will help you earn money.

I hope this book will lay a cornerstone for your successful crypto trading. In order to help you squeeze the most out of these pages, I developed practical homework assignments you can find after each section of the book. You can do them at any time convenient for you, but I ask you not to proceed to the next section before completing the task for the previous one.

Why? I will repeat (if you have not understood yet): trading is not about theory, it is about practice. Therefore, if you are lazy to practice every instrument you have read about, then after reading the book, you will gaze at the charts not being able to make heads or tails. This, in turn, will immediately lead to incorrect trading decisions and, hence, to financial losses. What do people tend to do in such cases? That's right, look for the guilty one. Do the homework assignments, learn your own best practices, and don't try to blame me for your misfortunes if you make bad decisions because you didn't practice.

I cannot perform the role of personal trainer, and I do not pursue this goal. I cannot stand next to your bed, pointing at the book with my forefinger, urging you to do your homework. It's up to you to decide whether you're going to do the tasks, therefore, the results also depend on you.

To sum up, I hope that my readers are future successful traders; therefore, they are ready to study and work a lot today for future gain.

So, I won't delay the start of your training, but want to note that this process should not be one-sided. Therefore, if you have benefited from my book, I will be grateful for your sincere feedback on Amazon. If you come up with any questions or do not find enough explanations in some section, feel free to email me. My assistant will structure all the questions and I will try to unveil more details in the next edition.

Are you ready to embark upon the training? Then let's go!

P.S. All the pictures in the book you can see in high quality here – bit.ly/pics-cpro

CHAPTER 1. UNDERSTANDING THE CRYPTOCURRENCY MARKET AND PSYCHOLOGY OF THE GAME

In order to understand the nature of trading in general and cryptocurrency trading in particular, we have to plunge into some financial processes, which we are all a part of.

Since we all use the banking sector services, and not only spend or place our well-earned money on deposit, but dreaming of a cloudless future late in life, transfer some part of the income to retirement funds, social security, and pensions, we automatically become participants of the banking system and the stock market. We pay pension contributions throughout life, but few of us think about the very structure of the financial industry and how the state disposes of our future pension.

Unfortunately, the financial system in any country is built in such a way that we do not own our capital. The circular motion of loans and pension contributions makes money somewhat virtual as they are constantly slipping through fingers of the state, fund managers, and private corporations. At the same time, central banks in any state exercise emission monopoly in respect of currency, and this function is assigned to them by the state. Theoretically, the currency is secured with goods or products produced in the territory of a country. This is how its GDP is formed. At the same time, central banks commit themselves to maintain the reliability and stability of the national currency.

It seems that everything is clear and good, but the problem is that it is just an ideal picture. Reality, unfortunately, is somewhat different. The state and central banks fail to fulfill their obligations to ensure the stability of the currency, and the value of money itself disappears due to inflation and quantitative easing. "How did it disappear? We were not informed about it!" you may mention rightfully. I'll try to substantiate my statement.

The value of money, including pension savings, and, therefore, the stability of our future, looked more optimistic before 1976. Until that time, the pension system worked as follows: people deposited money to the Pension Fund, interest was accrued on deposits, and the state used those funds to make payments. But the so-called Jamaica Accords[2] changed the course of history somewhat.

It was decided to demonetize gold, and gold turned into an ordinary exchange commodity. Thus, all the agreements approved within the framework of the Jamaica Accords allowed the price of gold to float with respect to the U.S. dollar and other currencies. It was a kind of call for many countries to get rid of gold. The

---

[2] The Jamaica Accords were a set of international agreements that ratified the end of the Bretton Woods monetary system

countries did not delay the relevant decision. A series of world countries decided to abandon this precious metal and not tie their national currency to the country's gold reserve.

I ask you to focus on this moment because since 1976 the credit system of each country has increased hundreds of thousands of times!

The Jamaica Accords turned money into figures. The system began to unify after the gold was abandoned, taking the form of huge unified bank accounts that are not backed up or guaranteed. As for the Pension Fund, it is no longer a kind of safe deposit box for your savings. It is a kind of hedge fund[3] that collects assets from you as an investor and then disposes of them at its discretion. Our pension funds became part of the state budget and started to be used for other government needs. Now the Pension Fund is a kind of bank account. If you analyze the pension system of the most developed world countries, you will find that pension funds are spent on other social needs. That's why pension deposits do not exist in an account somewhere.

Despite all these factors, the middle class has remained the driving force of the pension system, which is no longer supported by anything. Most people do not bother with how the Pension Fund disposes of money, so they keep replenishing its reserves. Like

---

[3] It is an investment fund that pools capital from accredited individuals or institutional investors and invests in a variety of assets, often with complex portfolio-construction and risk-management techniques. It is administered by a professional investment management firm, and often structured as a limited partnership, limited liability company, or similar vehicle.

bees in a hive they bring honey to the system regularly, but do not get to use this honey.

Doesn't it remind you of a pyramid? And I'm not talking about the pyramids in Egypt!

Let me mention that not only the pension system but the banking system as a whole, has the signs of this very pyramid scheme. All the participants in this system receive income only at the expense of inflow of "new blood", i.e., the receipt of new investments from new participants.

By the way, we've discussed the crisis of the financial system, but it should be noted that trading also experienced its hinge period. It is associated not with the Jamaica Accords in 1976, but with the global financial crisis of 2008. The crisis, as well as the availability of mobile systems and the prevalence of trading itself, stopped professional traders from earning exorbitant sums of money.

It is interesting that the crisis and the revolution in trading were organized by the world largest investment banks. Trying to deceive each other, they played a dishonest game, inventing various derivatives (promissory notes, bonds, etc.). Such products, invented by banks, began to confuse the situation in the market. The first wave of the fall hit the market in 1998, but then the situation was remedied. However, in 2008, even the reputation of a trader, who brings the whole system huge sums of money, could not prevent the market collapse and the start of a global economic crisis.

Thus, I believe that all the investment banks have discredited themselves as professional institutions that can be trusted to manage finances. That situation ended in real professional traders moving to hedge funds.

I believe it's high time to draw the first parallel between conventional (fiat) money and cryptocurrency. As we remember, the decisions taken within the framework of the Jamaica Accords made the value of money decrease significantly, because the entire currency cycle began to be built only on the foundation of debts. On the contrary, the value of cryptocurrency keeps growing. Moreover, cryptocurrency is not subject to inflation, since creation of new coins comes from a predictable algorithm, not a central bank..

Thus, if we ponder over the pension issue in the context of the above mentioned information, we can draw the following conclusions:

- You need to "mend your sails while the weather is fine", i.e., to think about a decent income in old age right now
- You need to look for an alternative to a pension

Trading could be one of such alternatives to a pension. However, the overwhelming majority of people bypass this option of earnings, because they believe this type of activity requires being a financial genius and having an innate talent for trading. People stuff their heads with such definitions as "pattern", "analysis", "technical modeling", "configurations of candlesticks" and, therefore, choose other, simpler, so they think, earning options.

But I want to cheer you up: being on close terms with all the above-mentioned concepts is a myth. In order to be successful in trading, you need to master the basic concepts of trading and the principles at work on exchanges. You only have to understand the main mechanics of the market: who sells and how and who buys and how. But you do not have to reinvent the wheel. Everything needed is already known.

Therefore, embarking upon the "profession" of a trader requires mastering the basic principles of the market, finding out how to analyze (i.e., assess the current situation), and, as a result, make trade decisions.

At the same time, I want to dispel the hopes of those newcomers who have already prepared their wallets for super profits but are going to devote a couple of hours a week to this matter. To become successful, which means getting a good income, you will have to constantly upgrade yourself, keep abreast of new methods, follow experienced traders, read the market news, etc. Therefore, freeloading won't do here, friends!

At the same time, traders have to stay cool and focused. Let me remind you that the cryptocurrency market is very volatile, but in spite of this, traders must make forecasts on the best time for entering and leaving the market. And all these risky operations have to be repeated again and again. Therefore, emotional poise is one of the trader's best friends. We will return to the psychology of a successful trader a couple more times.

Now let's touch briefly on the actors of cryptocurrency market. It is necessary to distinguish between two types of traders:

professional traders and retail traders. The first group includes those who have undergone special training and certification. As a rule, such people work in huge investment companies and speculate on the market with "tidy" sums of money. A retail trader carries out trading operations in the market without having a special license. Such people work for themselves and, as a rule, manage much smaller sums.

The downside of the work of professional traders is that they do not own the funds they manage. At the same time, professional traders punch a time clock, trying to survive in fierce competition. On the contrary, retail traders can make decisions at their discretion.

Since I consider my duty is not only to teach you but also to warn, I want to note that retail traders must always be ready to lose their capital as there is unspoken rule in the market called "90.90.90" which means that 90% of traders lose 90% of their capital in the first 90 days of work. All these lost funds do not dissolve. They stay in the market.

Understanding cryptocurrency market

Having dealt with all the pitfalls of banking and pension system, let's define: WHAT IS CRYPTOCURRENCY TRADING? I have three answers to this question for you:

- It's an opportunity to start to make money by investing in a cryptocurrency
- It's an opportunity to make a fortune in a short period of time

- It's a profitable instrument with little risk if traded correctly

My readers, knowing about my rich experience in this field, also often ask me the following questions:

- Is it worth investing in cryptocurrency now?
- Is it worth trading on the whole?
- Why should we analyze cryptocurrency?
- How do I invest without having experience?
- Is it better to invest yourself or entrust this to professionals?

I'm sure that all these questions have crossed your mind, but let's first start with basic principles.

Cryptocurrency[4] is a kind of digital currency, the creation, and control over which is based on cryptographic methods. As a rule, cryptocurrency uses decentralized control, i.e., there are no regulatory bodies in this field. The decentralized control of each cryptocurrency works through distributed ledger technology, typically a blockchain[5]. Information about transactions is usually not encrypted and is available in the public domain. To ensure the continuity of the chain of transaction blocks, the elements of

---

[4] A cryptocurrency (or crypto currency) is a digital asset designed to work as a medium of exchange that uses strong cryptography to secure financial transactions, control the creation of additional units, and verify the transfer of assets. Cryptocurrencies are a kind of alternative currency and digital currency (of which virtual currency is a subset).

[5] A blockchain, originally block chain, is a growing list of records, called blocks, which are linked using cryptography. Each block contains a cryptographic hash of the previous block, a timestamp, and transaction data (generally represented as a merkle tree root hash).

cryptography (digital signature based on a public key system) are used.

Now let me answer the question, why cryptocurrency is so important to me.

Cryptocurrency has remained the most profitable asset in recent years as well as the only asset a non-professional investor may use to increase their capital several-fold. You don't need outstanding knowledge, useful social contacts or huge initial investments.

It's a liberal and democratic asset which may boost your capital exponentially. That's the most attractive point of cryptocurrency for me. I think you will agree.

But, the most frequently asked question is: how can we use the opportunities cryptocurrency opens before us? Back in 2017, it was a little easier to take advantage of those opportunities. Many people yielded huge results by just investing in different coins. But the year 2018 began with the steep fall of the cryptocurrency. People started to look for other ways of benefiting from cryptocurrency. Trading is one such way.

On the one hand, its advantages are independence from the market and high profitability. For example, many trading companies showed fascinating financial results by the end of 2017. But do not hope the path of trading is easy (as it may seem to someone), it is also not fast. Therefore, you must understand there is a huge number of shortcomings and risks in trading. And the biggest risk for an inexperienced investor is that the outcome of trading depends on a qualitative analysis of the market situation and the assets you are to buy. It's difficult for a beginner. Although in 2017 the market still could be analyzed, now it is almost completely manipulative.

Some of you may wonder why analysis is so important in cryptocurrency trading. The analysis of cryptocurrency is needed to predict the behavior of a currency price in the market. It is the qualitative analysis that increases the probability of predicting the correct outcome of the transaction. If you were guessing would Bitcoin go up or down, say in the next two days, by tossing a coin, you would guess the right outcome only in 50% of cases. It is impossible to make a fortune this way. The analysis is needed to improve the quality of our guesses.

What do we want to guess?

- Entry point
- Take profit
- Stop loss (a limiter of losses that allows minimizing your losses and closing position if something goes wrong).

Now let's discuss it in more details.

What is an entry point? It's a cryptocurrency price at which we open a position. It is at this point where there are chances for the price to move in the forecast direction.

Take profit is the price at which we close the position with a profit. If everything goes according to plan, we are ready to say "Enough" at this point.

Stop loss is the level of "cutting off" losses is the price at which we will liquidate the position at a loss in case of an unfavorable change in price. For example, we expect a price to rise from 100 to 200, but it rises to 105 and then falls down. To avoid such situations, we set a price at which we want to liquidate the position if our forecast happens to be wrong.

To "guess" correctly more often, we apply three types of analysis:

- Fundamental
- Technical
- Computer

However, the types of analysis are one link in a chain. There is a need to understand the basic principles of market functioning. After all, if you don't have a clue about the internal mechanism of a car, you will not learn how to drive properly.

Therefore, to understand the cryptocurrency market, you need to know:

- Principles of cryptocurrency market monitoring
- The emergence of the cryptocurrency market, reasons for its success
- Forecast and development prospects
- Services and sites for traders
- Exchanges for trading
- Complete trading algorithm

We will deal with all of these issues in this book.

Psychology of the game

I'm ready to throw you a curve-ball again (here imagine broad laugh like in horror movies:)

So, if you think that having studied the market, the principles of fundamental and technical analysis you will become a successful trader, I will disappoint you - it is not enough.

You have forgotten about one very important aspect. To succeed in trading, you also need to understand the psychology of the game in the cryptocurrency market. Moreover, it is necessary to distinguish between the psychology of the game of crowd and the psychology of the game of market participants with large capital.

When working in mass speculative markets, an individual trader faces the following risks:

- Decisions of the crowd are made at the level of its most stupid member. So, the decisions taken by the crowd are not smart
- Rumors often control the crowd, and rumors tend not to be justified
- A person tends to be influenced by the crowd and make collective, non-individual decisions.

Therefore, to avoid such risks, you need to learn how to differentiate your individual transactions from the transactions you make following the example of the crowd. You need to try to become a kind of psychologist and feel the moment when your emotions could harm trading.

What emotions am I talking about?

The first emotion is greed.

Greed usually follows a sense of euphoria. It's a consequence of a certain experience. Let's say, you have got a very good interest on your deposit for the first time, so you fly into a passion. Subsequently, you make another bet - and you are lucky again. After that, take my word for it, you won't listen to anyone. You will treat any sound idea in your environment about a need to stop an absolute delirium. And why? Because you have started to feel greedy!

And how does greed manifest itself in the cryptocurrency market? Many traders hope to buy currency at the lowest price and sell at the highest, i.e., they do not look for a point to lock their profits but keep a coin, hoping its price will grow endlessly.

Tip: if you have an opportunity to close a deal and reap a benefit now, you'd better do it rather than hoping for luck and keep waiting.

The second emotion is hope and expectation.
After you fell into a trap of greed, you start to feel hope and expectation.

In particular, those people who have come to the market with confidence that here they will earn millions of dollars hope that things will work out for them in the long run with little effort. Unfortunately, it is not as simple as it seems at first glance. To make money here, you will have to work your tail off.

When do hope and expectation appear in the cryptocurrency market? When you hope without any grounds and await a price reverse.

Tip: you need to understand why price should reverse

(using all kinds of analysis), rather than hope and wait.

The third emotion is fear.

In most cases, this emotion arises from ignorance or misunderstanding what should be expected. For example, you are afraid of the dark, but if truth be told, you are afraid of not knowing what could hide in the dark. Therefore, the fear arises when you do not have answers to certain questions.

When does fear appear in the cryptocurrency market? It appears when the currency price begins to fall. And the lower the price falls, the greater the fear you feel.

What do traders do when they are seized with fear? Some continue making new purchases, using moving average strategy, while others close positions after the first decline. However, there is a third category of people: they do nothing except looking entranced at the chart.

Tip: there's nothing worse than looking at the falling price. If you start to feel fear at a certain moment of trading and you make unplanned moves, determine the cause of fear and cut it off.

In order to open and close all positions "on schedule", be sure to keep a **trader's diary**. If you think it is easy to remember all the transactions and you don't need a trader's diary, you choose a far from professional approach towards trading which leads you to the repeated mistakes.

Therefore, when trading, you need to turn off your emotions as they will have an impact on your chart (technical analysis) in one way or another. Think not only as an analyst but as a psychologist as well. Identify emotions in the early stages and cut them off in time.

To understand the psychology of the market, you will also need to study some of its **laws**, a certain list of rules revealed in the market.

The law of chance. You never know what can happen the next moment, so always be ready for everything - both to large returns and losses. Therefore, take into account possible accidents when making your market calculations.

Sod's law. You can make perfect calculations and forecast and receive seemingly 100% confirmation, but someone changes the rules of the game when you make a deal. Never forget about such a probability. Be ready to change the rules of the game.

Law of optimism. People are inclined to exaggerate the chances of winning. This exaggeration can press you for making deals on the most unthinkable and the first offered prices. Sometimes your worst enemy is yourself!

The law of cause and effect. If you observe any movement, then try to find the reason that caused it. I highly recommend not making any deals without understanding what makes the price move one direction or another. There is no movement without a reason.

Whales in the world of crypto

You have probably heard that the cryptocurrency market is "inhabited" with hamsters, whales and many other species of animals. This may sound ridiculous, but it's true. Imagine the cryptocurrency market is the ocean. Consequently, the usual traders are small fish in it, the pumping groups are sharks and the largest asset owners are whales. The whales are believed to control the cryptocurrency market and be able to collapse it any moment. But is it so, and can ordinary investors (like us) benefit from the actions of whales? Let's see!

Who are the whales in the cryptocurrency market?

Whales are large players who own huge amounts of cryptocurrency and can manage the market by buying up and selling assets.

Such whales harbor even in the ordinary stock market, but they have many more opportunities in the cryptocurrency market:

- Cryptocurrency market capitalization (about $300 billion) is much smaller, so it is much easier to accumulate a large number of coins in your hands than to try to become a whale in a conventional market (with a capitalization of $65 trillion)
- Whales can manage large sums without feeling any pressure from banks and financial regulators, as there is no large-scale regulation despite the realities of tightening state control over cryptocurrency
- The cryptocurrency market is still very young and operates according to the laws not typical in the traditional market. A cryptocurrency's price is determined by demand, and large asset holders can manipulate it.

The main characteristic of whales is that they own large amounts of cryptocurrency and their main goal is to manage the price of this cryptocurrency for the sake of their own benefit. To this end, a coin should be very popular and in demand.

Every day, thousands of small fish (ordinary investors) pour their money into the common ocean, while whales are reaping their benefit. That is why the Bitcoin market is of particular interest for such whales.

Let's now sort out what kinds of whales live in the cryptocurrency market:

- Early adopters of Bitcoin, who were first to mine or buy up huge amounts of coins and now have thousands or even tens of thousands of Bitcoin on their accounts
- Wealthy investors, who managed to buy large amounts of Bitcoin in the early days of its popularity
- Large investment and hedge funds
- Large companies who can buy or mine a large number of coins to their own benefit (for example, cryptocurrency exchanges or producers of mining equipment).

According to the latest data, at the time of writing, about 80% of all mined Bitcoin belonged to 110 people. They are the whales who have real levers of influence on the market price of Bitcoin.

Here is a small list of the most famous Bitcoin whales:

- Roger Ver (150,000 BTC)
- Binance exchange (160,000 BTC)
- Bitfinex exchange (190,000 BTC)

- Bitmain company (350,000 BTC)
- Winklevoss twins (450,000 BTC)
- Bitcoin creator Satoshi Nakamoto (he is said to own a million coins).

If you think that only Bitcoin is concentrated in the hands of a narrow circle of whales, you are mistaken. The same is true for other types of cryptocurrency. For example, 40% of all Ethereum coins are located in top 100 crypto wallets of this coin. With cryptocurrencies Qtum, Gnosis, and Storj, this figure reaches 90%.

Bitcoin whales are the most influential in the market because bitcoin has the highest capitalization and market value of any coin.

Despite all these facts, I hear almost daily the exclamations of skeptics that no whales exist, and a small group of people cannot manage the price of cryptocurrency. But the facts remain facts and speak for themselves. People with a colossal amount of cryptocurrency in their wallets can manage the whole market.

So which strategies do whales use in the cryptocurrency market?
I'll highlight several strategies whales use in the cryptocurrency market.

Rinse and repeat. The main trick of this strategy is to reduce the price for a particular cryptocurrency as much as possible to be able to buy it at the lowest price a little bit later. Implementing this strategy is like taking candy from a baby: whale sells its assets on a massive scale at a price below the market one, and the ordinary small fish, scared by a cryptocurrency collapse, also starts to sell their assets. As a result, the price of cryptocurrency falls even lower, and then the whale buys coins at this fallen price. The large-scale purchase makes the price rise again, and the whale repeats its cycle.

Here is an example. A whale has 10,000 BTC. The current price is $6,000, and the whale sets orders to sell Bitcoin for $5,800. Suppose he "throws away" 6,000 BTC in the market. Having noticed this, ordinary traders decide that Bitcoin follows the downtrend or collapses. Accordingly, they start to get rid of their assets. If it becomes massive (that is what the whales are trying to achieve), the Bitcoin price may drop to $5,000 or even lower. In this case, the whale will return his 6,000 BTC, which he had previously sold, and would buy more coins at a reduced price.

And now let's count. The whale sold his 6,000 BTC for $34 million. If the price collapses to $5,000, he will be able to buy 7,000 BTC for this money. That is, his dirty profit will total $5 million. That's just one "rinse" round, and the whale is interested in "rinsing" as many coins from ordinary traders as possible.

Spoofing. The main purpose of a whale in this strategy is to make other players believe in a collapse or growth of a particular cryptocurrency. To do this, the whale does not even need to throw away his own assets in the market as it's enough to place large orders on the exchange and cancel them before they are executed. Moreover, this strategy involves both buy and sell orders.

In the first case, whale places an order to buy a large amount of cryptocurrency (for example, Bitcoin), thereby increasing the sell wall. Other traders see it and begin to buy Bitcoin massively, expecting a price hike. The whale waits until the price reaches its peak, cancels the order and sells part of its assets at an overvalued price.

In the second case, whale places an order to sell a large amount of Bitcoin at a price below the market value. Ordinary traders hit the panic button and dump their assets. The whale waits for the maximum price drop, cancels his order, and buys Bitcoin.

The main point of this strategy is to place orders that cannot be executed.

For example, if a whale sells 10,000 BTC at a low price, and the rest of the traders have enough money to buy them, the whale will simply lose his assets. If traders fail to buy out the entire amount, the rest of the players will either have to wait until the order is executed or reduce the sale price themselves. And that's playing into the whale's hand.

Over-the-counter game. Some experts believe that many whales in the cryptocurrency market trade assets in the over-the-counter (OTC) market. It's a kind of black market where the whales can buy a huge amount of coins out of public view. Non-public trading is carried out in closed groups, through major OTC brokers or at the exchanges that offer so-called "private rates." The brokers, who offer their customers lower prices and work only with the largest players, are of particular interest to whales.

For example, well-known Circle and Cumberland over-the-counter brokers have restricted access for new entrants: $100,000 is the fee for entering the circle of favorites, $250,000 - for cryptocurrency trading.

Working through such brokers, whales can buy cryptocurrency from each other and even coordinate their actions. Having bought a large number of coins, they go to ordinary exchanges and influence the cryptocurrency price as they need.

It may seem that the whales are high-ranking pumpers. However, it's not so. Pumpers raise the altcoin price suitable for Pump & Dump[6]. They kick up a fuss in the cryptocurrency community, manipulate news hooks, gather pump groups to purchase coins, and so on. Whales, however, sway the market towards the preferential price of an asset they hold. They also act together often, and the main target of most whales is Bitcoin. Little-known altcoins do not interest them.

How do the whales influence the cryptocurrency market?

Many investors believe that whales have a negative impact on the cryptocurrency market, depriving small players of their profits. Moreover, the cryptocurrency community has long discussed the conspiracy theories saying whales want to either collapse the entire market or to secure their own total control over it. Let's try to answer this question by analyzing the arguments of conspiracy theorists.

---

[6] **Pump and dump" (P&D)** is a form of securities fraud that involves artificially inflating the price of an owned stock through false and misleading positive statements, in order to sell the cheaply purchased stock at a higher price. Once the operators of the scheme "dump" sell their overvalued shares, the price falls and investors lose their money. This is most common with small cap cryptocurrencies and very small corporations.

For example, here is one theory: whales are stocking up with Bitcoin to control the market after the mining era ends. According to calculations, all Bitcoin will be mined within 5-6 years, and the developers will have to transfer the network to PoS-mining[7], which means that the largest coin holders – the whales – will benefit the most from PoS rewards. Nowadays, many people claim that the *Bitcoin collapse, which began in the winter of 2018, was triggered by whales.* They are already preparing for PoS-mining and are doing everything they can to buy as many coins as possible. However, due to the collapse of the Bitcoin price, a huge number of users left, while many potential investors have not entered it, waiting for the next fall. Bitcoin started to follow a downward trend, and this affected not only the ordinary trader's pocket.

In fact, the whales need cryptocurrency to be popular and in demand with the largest possible number of players. After all, when whales' assets fall in price, their portfolios also get cheaper. In the long run, it is unprofitable for them to collapse the cryptocurrency.

However, there are other opinions about the whales in the cryptocurrency market. Some say they are not a negative phenomenon. Such players exist in any market. They always set the vector of development and unite to lead the market. Therefore, whales, to some extent, even exert a positive influence on the

---

[7] **Proof of stake (PoS)** is a type of algorithm by which a cryptocurrency blockchain network aims to achieve distributed consensus. In PoS-based cryptocurrencies the creator of the next block is chosen via various combinations of random selection and wealth or age (*i.e.,* the stake).

market. After all, while they are interested in the cryptocurrency they hold, they are also interested in preventing the collapse.

Moreover, many whales (including Nakamoto) do not even use their assets in order to lower or raise the cryptocurrency price. They keep coins in their wallets, maintaining a balance in the market.

It should be mentioned that even those whales who play with the sell walls and rinse Bitcoin can be useful for an ordinary investor. To use them for your benefit, you need to catch the wave they created.

How can an ordinary investor profit from whales' actions?
Yes, you've understood right. You can benefit from whales. It is a wave created by a whale which is an ideal opportunity to enter the market. For example, when a whale goes bear and places orders to sell huge amounts of cryptocurrency at a price lower than the market, the price naturally falls. Most traders start to sell their assets, but it would be much cleverer to start to buy them as a whale does. When a whale increases the buy wall and other traders start to buy cryptocurrency, raising the price, it's high time to sell your assets.

Here, the most important nuance is being able to notice a whale's trend in time. There are two ways to do this:

- To monitor the movement of funds (in particular, Bitcoin) on the largest cryptocurrency wallets. You can do this on www.bitinfocharts.com . A large transfer from the wallet indicates that a whale is throwing his assets in the market, which means we must wait for price changes. If it falls sharply, it makes sense to buy up cryptocurrency quickly, if it suddenly jumps - to sell. The clearest signal is when transfers are made from several top wallets.

- To follow the order book on top-level cryptocurrency exchanges. Placement of orders to buy or sell huge amounts of cryptocurrency is mostly linked with games of whales. If you see an overvalued buy wall, do not rush to buy coins. It's better to wait for the peak and sell your assets at a beneficial price. If a whale maintains a semblance of collapse (by overvaluing sell wall), wait for a serious recession and buy coins. After all, soon a whale will buy them cheap and raise the price.

I'll give you a piece of advice: if you are an inexperienced trader, don't follow the whale trends. To play like them, you need to think like them. You should be able to determine the overvalued buy and sell walls, analyze the overall situation in the market, and correctly assess the situation on the exchanges. If you have such skills, you will be able to generate profits.

Prospects for cryptocurrency market development

Have you ever wondered why cryptocurrency is becoming more and more popular? It's largely because the purchasing power of fiat money keeps dropping. This process is driven by two main factors:

- An increasing number of people learn about Bitcoin and come to the conclusion it is the most promising currency
- Liquidity grows. Buying Bitcoin today requires much less money and effort than a year ago.

In my opinion, these factors can even provoke hyperbitcoinization.

Hyperbitcoinization may occur if the world governments decide to tighten the screws in the cryptocurrency market and attempt to control capital. Bitcoin will have a chance to become currency No.1. After all, it has no borders, and it does not depend on patriotism or ethnicity of a person. Although the use of Bitcoin is based not on physical properties, like gold and silver, but on mathematical properties, it has all the characteristics of money (durability, mobility, divisibility) and can fully perform its functions (means of accumulation, payment, etc.). The real price for Bitcoin is determined by the balance between the demand of people who need it and the supply of people who own it.

To conclude this section, I want to say the following: if your decision to master cryptocurrency trading is firm and irreversible, then I do not recommend seeking the help of professional traders. Each of them, of course, can promise to explain simple and effective trading strategies. However, one must understand that a professional trader won't demonstrate their methods of analysis, charts or reveal personal secrets to an outsider. Therefore, the path of a retail trader by trial and error is much shorter and more profitable. You already completed the first step when you bought my book. ☺

Homework

Choose 5 cryptocurrencies you would like to trade, study them and write down their features:

- Capitalization
- Exchanges they are traded on
- Trading volume
- Technological solutions of a coin
- Coin creators' Twitter accounts
- Location of head office
-

CHAPTER 2. CHOOSING AN EXCHANGE AND A PLATFORM FOR TECHNICAL ANALYSIS

After a basic insight into the guts of the cryptocurrency market and psychology of the game of its participants, the next step on the path of your rapprochement with trading will be registering on an exchange. The exchange is the king in trading. We trust it with our money. We visit it day and night to check the depth of the market and execution of orders, etc.

Don't get intimidated with the importance of choosing a perfect exchange. I warn you: it does not exist. Each exchange currently operating in the cryptocurrency market has its pros and cons. So, do not look for an ideal one, seek the one which will meet your requirements: simplicity and user-friendly interface, a large number of trading pairs, prompt technical support and so on. I will give you two tips:

- Choose among top 10 best exchanges
- Register accounts on at least two exchanges to diversify your risks.

It's easy enough to get registered on an exchange. But still, let me walk you through all the stages of registering and depositing funds on one of the exchanges. This process is almost identical for all exchanges, so you can repeat similar actions on any other exchange.

Let's take the Binance exchange (www.binance.com) as an example.

If you only want to follow the market situation on Binance, you do not need to register. However, if you aim to make transactions, you need to create an account and perform a number of simple actions.

Go to the official website www.binance.com, select the interface language and click "Register".

When registering, use a strong unique password.

Register

| ✉ Email |
| 🔒 Password |
| 🔒 Confirm Password |
| 👤 Referral ID (optional) |

☐ I agree to Binance's Terms of Use

Register

Already Registered? Log In

Having entered the data, check the box indicating you agree to the terms of use and proceed to the next step. You will need to drag the slider to fit a puzzle piece.

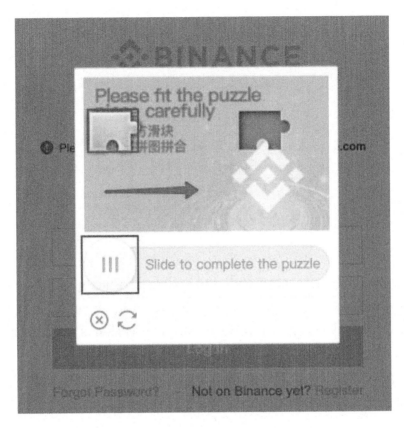

Afterward, open the verification email and click on the link. Now you can log into Binance account using your email and password.

Our registration is almost complete. But! I recommend that you also enable two-factor authentication.

So, the first time you start, you have to confirm that you are familiar with the security recommendations. You just need to check each box for activating "I understand, continue" button.

Next, you will be recommended to enable two-factor authentication using the Google Authenticator key or confirmations via SMS. Two-factor authentication is a simple and effective way to prevent unauthorized access. You can postpone this procedure by pressing "Skip for now", but I recommend enabling it immediately.

We strongly recommend you to enable 2FA on your account !

Please choose how you wish to receive 2FA code:

 Google Authentication  SMS Authentication

I understand the risks for not enabling 2FA   Skip for now

You can use your account to:

- Change the password for entering the exchange
- Enable two-factor authentication and complete verification
- Get API key for automation of trading with the help of bots
- View transaction history and list of recent IP addresses used to enter the exchange.

Please note that no verification is required for trading on the exchange or depositing and withdrawing money. Still, you will be able to raise the withdrawal limit from 2 BTC to 100 BTC per day only after enabling of two-factor authentication and verification of user data (you need to fill out the form: name, address, etc., as well as attach scans of a passport and a picture of you holding your passport).

SMS confirmation and verification are as simple and intuitive as possible, so I will not explain them in detail.

Next, you will want to deposit funds into your account on the exchange. Depositing is possible only with cryptocurrency - you cannot enter or withdraw fiat money, like on many other large exchanges. For this reason, verification is not an indispensable prerequisite for trading on the exchange. At the stage of making the first deposit, you will get a deposit address for the selected cryptocurrency. (1) Copy it to avoid mistakes when typing (2) or scan with a phone when depositing via a mobile app (3). The number of necessary network confirmations for depositing the cryptocurrency to the account is indicated below. (4) For example, to deposit BTC you need two confirmations.

Important

- Send only **BTC** to this deposit address. Sending any other coin or token to this address may result in the loss of your deposit.

BTC Deposit Address

1LdRSNU3btxUY4WVpQhXHeQst2AWbH6hsJ

Please note

- Coins will be deposited immediately after 2 network confirmations
- After making a deposit, you can track its progress on the history page.

Be careful: the cryptocurrency chosen for depositing into the trading account must coincide with the one you send to the exchange. Depositing of one type of cryptocurrency into the wallet of another cryptocurrency can lead to losses of your funds. For your first time, I recommend using a small amount to make sure that everything works well!

After you've registered, deposited funds into your account and familiarized yourself with the exchange interface, don't hesitate to start to trade. The process of trading on Binance exchange is basically the same as on other exchanges. Having grasped the principles at work with orders on this exchange, you can trade on any other exchange.

Three types of orders are available for buying or selling cryptocurrency: Limit, Market and Stop-Limit. All types of orders offer the option of a quick setting of the amount of purchased or sold cryptocurrency: 25-100% of all available assets for the selected cryptocurrency pair. For example, if you select "25%" for "Buy Order" in AION/BTC pair, you will buy AION to the tune of 25% of the BTC you have. If you select 25%" for "Sell Order", you will sell 25% of AION coins in stock.

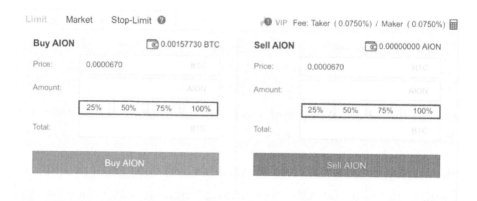

Newcomers often do not understand: why do we need two types of limit orders? The answer lies in the specifics of their execution. After all, due to the specifics of cryptocurrency, you cannot set Take Profit (exact price at which to close out an open position for a profit) or Stop Loss (designed to **limit** an investor's **loss** on a position) with one order.

All these new terms can be confusing for a beginner, so let's look at a simple example.

Market Order
To make it simple, let's start with a market order, which is a request to buy or sell a security at the best available price in the current market. In this case, you need to choose to buy or sell, enter the amount of cryptocurrency needed for execution and click "Buy" or "Sell" button. After an order opens, the system will automatically try to execute an order at the most favorable price for a trader. Let's look at how orders are executed at a market price.

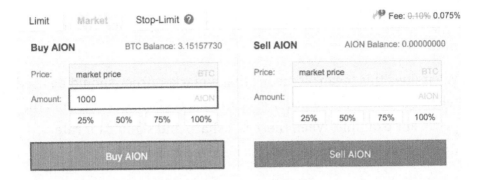

For example, we opened an order to buy 1,000 units of cryptocurrency. At the time we opened the order to buy, somebody else had already placed an order to sell cryptocurrency at the price that we deemed acceptable for purchase. Since it's the lowest price on the market, the exchange will automatically purchase all AION available at that price for us, up to 1000 AION (our total order).

But if the order volume at the lowest price is less than our order, the system will only partially execute the order at price No.1, and the rest of the order will be executed at the slightly higher price No.2 of the next sell order on the market. This second price is slightly worse for us than the initial one.

If the volume of this order to sell at the price No. 2 is also not enough to fully execute our order, the rest of the order will be executed at the price No.3 of the sale order in the depth of market, which is again slightly worse for us than the previous one. This will repeat until the order is fully executed (e.g. 1000 AION).

The larger the volume of our order is, the lower trading volume for the selected currency pair is, and the stronger the rate fluctuation is, the bigger difference between the final strike price and the initial one will be.

What does this mean? It means that a market order should be used when the speed of the order execution is more important than the price. For example, when there is a sharp and significant rate fluctuation and the movement is believed to go on.

Limit Order

And if there is a price reversal, and you want to sell or buy a coin at the best price and at the same time minimize losses as much as possible? Limit orders allow you to make a trading operation with execution at the initial price or even at the price which is better than you indicate. Let me explain using the example.

Suppose the current price for an AION coin is 0.0003815 BTC. We anticipate a price correction - decline with the subsequent resumption of growth. We want to buy 1,000 AION when the price drops to 0.0003500. We select a limit order and enter the data for the order: (1) the price at which we will buy (0.00035), and the number of coins we want to buy (1,000 AION). The trading panel will automatically calculate the needed number of Bitcoin on the account - 0.35 BTC – to execute the order (2). If the market reaches the indicated price and there will be no sufficient amount on the balance, the order will not be executed.

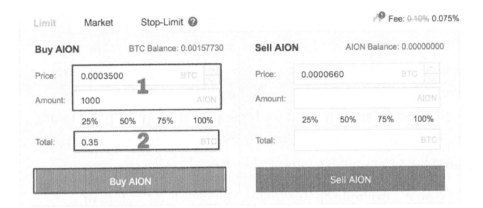

What happens next?

If the market does not reach the indicated price, for example, the price reverses at 0.0003550, the order will remain inactive and, subsequently, we will have to delete it. But if the market still reaches the indicated price, there are three possible case scenarios:

1) Market reaches the price and even crosses it. It means there is enough volume to close our order. In this case, the order is filled, and we receive the desired 1,000 AION at 0.00035, or, perhaps, even for the better price. In this case, you can place a limit order to sell AION at a profit;

2) Market reaches the price, activates our order, but the volume is too small, and our order is executed partially. After that, the price reverses and goes much higher than 0.00035. This means that the order remains to be open; we receive only a part of the quantity indicated in the order but for a price no worse we indicated. Afterwards, we should either wait for the full execution of the order or close it, being happy with what we have already bought;

3) Market reaches the price, crosses it, our order is filled. However, instead of the expected price increase, it keeps falling, and at some point, it becomes obvious that we goofed up. As a rule, we realize that it's better to sell the purchased cryptocurrency with a small loss than wait for large drawdown when it's already too late to correct something. To avoid this, we really need to place Stop Loss to minimize potential losses.

The above example shows that we need to limit orders to maximize profits. However, such pending orders may trigger losses if the forecasts turn out to be erroneous. One of the differences between trading in the cryptocurrency market and trading in classical financial markets is the impossibility of simultaneous placement of Take Profit and Stop Loss in one order. Therefore, stop limit orders come to the rescue.

Stop Limit in the capacity of Take Profit

Stop-Limit orders work similarly to conventional limit orders, but with an additional condition. Placing a pending Stop-Limit order, a trader specifies additional stop price, which the market price should hit for activating a pending limit price and add it to the common depth of market. Stop-Limit order is filled like a limit order, within the specified price range, indicated by the stop price and limit price. The order is executed only between the stop price and limit price if there are suitable orders in the depth of the market. If the market price crosses the limit price before the full execution of the order, it may not be filled.

To make it clear, let's take a chart with strong fluctuations, for example, an XRP / U.S. dollar pair.

We stay at the current price level, *marked in №1*. There is an upward reversal on the chart, determined by the head and shoulders pattern, but we decide to wait for confirmation of the upward trend at a level we indicate as stop price. If market price hits our stop price, our forecast will be confirmed and our order will be activated. At the same time, we realize that the price can rebound from the indicated stop price and go in the opposite direction. After all, the market price can cross or rebound from the price we set.

If the market price hits the stop price, the order is activated, and we buy cryptocurrency within the corridor limited by stop price and limit price. At the same time, if the market price temporarily falls, testing the level of resistance, it allows buying at more favorable prices. But if the market price hits the limit price and keeps falling, the purchase of cryptocurrency stops. Thus, Stop-Limit orders allow a trader to buy only the cryptocurrency whose value is growing.

Stop Limit in the capacity of Stop Loss

Apart from safety reasons, Stop-Limit orders are used as stop losses. Let's take the same chart. Now we intend to wait for the price drop and buy cryptocurrency at the most favorable price before another spike.

We set a limit order to buy below the market price. But how to protect ourselves against losses if the price suddenly continues to fall after our limit order is triggered? A standard limit order cannot perform the function of Stop Loss level, since setting a sell order with a price below the market price will result in the sale of available assets at a market price as the system perceives it as more profitable for sale. Remember? Buy low, sell high...

Therefore, we set a Stop-Limit order at a Stop Loss level like in the previous figure, and now its task will be not to maximize profits, but to minimize losses. Accordingly, we set the limit price at the Stop Loss level, while we set the stop price, which activates this order, slightly lower. Why should we do this?

The order will not be executed until the market price reaches the stop price, and when it reaches it, the limit price of the sell order ("sell at this price or lower") will not allow selling the cryptocurrency, if the price suddenly goes up in the direction we need. In addition, it will not prevent us from selling the asset when the price moves down, acting like Stop Loss and minimizing losses.

I hope that this guideline helped you understand how to register and deposit money for trading on the Binance exchange. Let me remind you that the cryptocurrency market is fast-changing and some items may change at the time you read the book. In any case, you understand the basic principles and will be able to apply them to other exchanges.

The Top 10 Exchanges

Now I will try to simplify your life a little by narrowing the list of exchanges that can become your trading platform. I will identify top 10 best exchanges, pointing to their strong and weak points. These ten exchanges are the best at the time me writing this book because of the largest number of presented cryptocurrency pairs.

If the statistics on these exchanges alters with time, the essence will remain the same.

1. HitBTC (Estonia)
2. Bittrex (United States)
3. Binance (Japan)
4. Poloniex (United States)
5. OKEx (China)
6. Huobi (China)
7. Bitfinex (Honk Kong)
8. Kraken (United States)
9. Bitstamp (Luxembourg)
10. Bithumb (South Korea).

When choosing an exchange, weigh all the pros and cons, do not be lazy to devote time to this as it's about your money. Let's now highlight the pros and cons of some exchanges.

Bithumb

Pros:

- Relatively low fees (0.15%)
- High liquidity
- Unique opportunity to buy gift certificates/vouchers

Cons:

- Interface
- Was subjected to cyber attacks
- Korean language mostly, only a little information is available in English

- All currency pairs are tied only to South Korean won. Therefore, if you have only Bitcoin and want to buy, for example, Ethereum, you will have to buy wons
- Fixed fees, not tied to trade volume
- Just few trading pairs are available

Poloniex

Pros:

- Quick account creation
- Multitasking functionality (margin trading with 2.5x leverage, possibility to provide and get loans)
- High liquidity
- User-friendly interface (navigation, sorting, quick search, night-vision function, etc.)
- Relatively low fees
- API, two-factor authentication 2FA;
- Technical analysis tools (Fibonacci levels, moving averages, Bollinger bands)

Cons:

- Slow customer service
- No mobile application
- No fiat currency support. The dollar exchange rate is tied to altcoin Tether (USDT), which costs exactly $1, but in crisis times its rate does not always correspond to the dollar

Bitfinex

Pros:

- Multitasking functionality (margin trading with up to 3.3x leverage, possibility to provide and get loans)
- High liquidity
- Different fees: for a market maker - 0.1% and lower with an increase in turnover; for a market taker - 0.2% or lower
- API, two-factor authentication 2FA, advanced verification tools to monitor the accounting integrity
- Customizable interface (theme selection, sorting)
- Technical analysis tools embedded in TradingView
- Mobile apps for iOS and Android
- A large number of orders (stop loss, take profit and others).

Cons:

- When depositing funds into the wallet or withdrawing funds via bank transfer in USD, the exchange charges fees of 0.1%, but not less than $20. Therefore it is better to make cryptocurrency deposits
- Complicated verification

Kraken

Pros:

- Good reputation, high liquidity
- For corporate clients. In addition, a corporate program is provided to customers, who carry out transactions with a large amount of cash
- Possibility to deposit various types of fiat currency and cryptocurrency into the wallet

- API, two-factor authentication, possibility to apply advanced security settings
- The possibility of margin trading, several types of orders
- Relatively low transaction fees
- Application for iOS
- Excellent customer support

Cons:

- An absence of intuitive user interface
- High fees for depositing a wallet and withdrawing funds
- More suitable for advanced traders

Bittrex

Pros:

- Possibility to create anonymous accounts
- Friendly, minimalist interface
- Technical analysis tools
- API, two-factor authentication
- High-level security has never been hacked

Cons:

- Fees of 0.25% for all transactions. No reductions as turnover grows
- Sometimes liquidity is below average and execution of order can last about 10 minutes
- No margin trading
- When creating an anonymous account, there are higher withdrawal limits (up to $50,000) as well as only cryptocurrency deposits and withdrawals
- Many users are unhappy with the technical support team

Tradingview online technical analysis platform

Before you give a person wings, you need to teach how to use them. Therefore, before we proceed to the study of technical analysis, I should teach my reader how to use the necessary tools on the Tradingview online technical analysis platform. If such information seems too basic for you, do not worry, skip this section and move on. I devote this section to those readers who make their very first steps in trading and are not yet familiar with the needed services and platforms.

Tradingview (www.tradingview.com) is a social network for traders based on an online platform for technical analysis. Here you can not only draw your own charts but also to follow other traders and monitor their forecasts.

In order to switch to charts on this platform, we click on the Chart button on the homepage. Now consider the top panel above the chart. We will move from left to right.

A **cryptocurrency pair** is in the far left corner. The **timeframe** is next to the right. The timeframe is a time interval within which one candle is formed.

Further on the panel, we can choose the **type of chart**. Personally, I prefer Japanese candlestick. Traders began to use the technical analysis of Japanese candlestick in the 17th century, almost from the very beginning of the exchange trade. But you can choose bars or other types of charts.

The next button on the panel is **"Compare"**. Here we can compare different assets and check whether there is a correlation between assets on a chart.

Then we can choose an indicator. Each of them has its pros and cons. But thanks to the indicators, we can understand whether the market is overbought or oversold.

The second button on the right above the chart will allow you to save or download your forecasts.

In order to set up your chart, we click on a gearwheel in the right corner, and the main menu of the schedule settings will open. Here we can change the style (background, color of candlesticks, etc.); scale (all that is related to the scale, size and values of the chart); background shading and other functions.

Now let's look at the panel to the left of the chart.

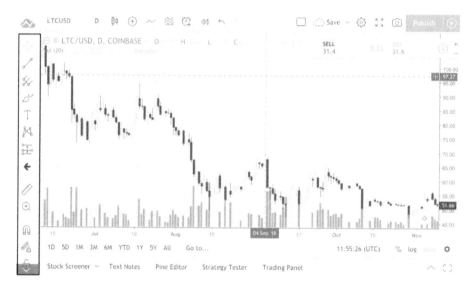

The first button is a type of cursor. Below there are technical analysis tools. Let's consider the trend line because you will often use this tool.

What is this line for? It is needed to determine the trend and to find a turning point on the existing trend. To apply this line, you must have at least two points. We find them, stretch the line, clone it and place it parallel to the first line.

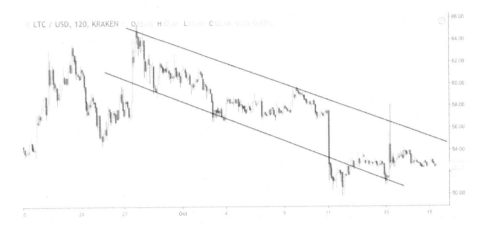

Advanced graphic tools are located under the third button of the left vertical panel. There are a lot of them here, but the **Fibonacci** retracement is most often used. This tool will help you to determine possible retracement goals; possible goals of trend continuation; strong support and resistance levels.

By pressing the fourth button on the left panel, you will be able to draw various shapes. A brush is also available here.

The fifth button provides text elements and arrows.

The sixth button offers different patterns, for example, the Head and shoulders pattern.

The seventh button offers the forecasting tools. For example, we can measure the height of graphic figures with the help of "Price range" tool.

If you want to remove the drawn figure from your chart, then click on the lowest button on the panel. If you want to locally delete only one tool or line, then click on it and you will have a menu of options.

Also, you have the opportunity to hide the forecast you drawn on the chart. To do this, press the button with an eye.

And finally, let's consider the panel to the right of the chart.

A menu of quotes is at the top. It is a very convenient feature that allows storing all the assets that you work with. To select the desired asset, enter the first letters of the currency in the search bar. You will have a menu for selection. Here you choose not only the cryptocurrency but also the exchange which you will trade it on.

The last function, which is useful for me personally and for you as well, is the alarm clock icon. It helps to create alerts to track price movements. But keep in mind that this function works only when your computer is turned on.

Practice drawing charts every day, track your forecast and improve your trading skills. Using Tradingview is a skill that you'll improve over time and as you learn the technical indicators in the rest of this book.

Homework

1) Choose at least two cryptocurrency exchanges for trading, get registered on them and deposit funds into a trading account
2) Get registered on Tradingview platform and gain insight on its functionality

CHAPTER 3. DEVELOPING A TRADING ALGORITHM

For any work to be structured and, therefore, successful, we must develop a clear algorithm of actions. Trading is no exception. For example, we cannot start cryptocurrency trading without registering on the exchange or learning how to work with the Tradingview platform. Everything should be done in due order.

Of course, every trader has their own unique path and tailored algorithm of actions. However, as time passes and we gain experience, the sequence of your actions in trading can change. However, we should always have a certain algorithm. This will help save time and avoid financial losses.

So, if you need a basic and a short algorithm to start trading, you're welcome. Take a pen and write it down.

1. Create a cryptocurrency wallet
2. Create an account on Tradingview platform and learn its tools
3. Register an account on the exchange (it's better to get registered on several exchanges) and undergo verification

4. Determine the ways of depositing and withdrawing funds from the exchange
5. Study the process of placing orders on the exchange
6. Create our own trading strategy
7. Start independent trading

This algorithm is shallow, but you still can use it and adjust to your needs and preferences.

And now, my young traders, let's look at this algorithm with a fine-tooth comb and analyze the early stages of your trading in details.

1. Reviewing the cryptocurrency market dynamics
So, the first thing every self-respecting trader should do before they start to trade is to analyze the current situation on the world financial markets. Try to identify the most prevalent activities.

After you find the answers to these questions, determine which coins, based on the information previously received, could be profitable now.

2. Choosing the coins
The determining factors in the process of choosing a coin should be its volatility and liquidity.

Volatility is a statistical financial indicator that characterizes the volatility of a price. It's a crucial indicator in the management of financial risks.

Liquidity[8] describes the degree to which an asset or security can be quickly bought or sold in the market without affecting the asset's price. Liquidity is measured with the number of trades executed (trade volume) and the spread value – the difference between the maximum bid and the minimum ask price of a security or asset (you can see this in a depth of market, which I will characterize a little bit later). So, the more transactions are executed and less the spread the value is, the higher the liquidity is.

3. Exploring the chosen tools for trading - technical and fundamental analyses

Technical and fundamental analyses are the main methods of evaluating the market as a whole and types of cryptocurrency in particular.

Fundamental analysis helps us to determine the general trends and situation in the market, while technical analysis helps to choose the best moments for opening and closing a position.

Put it differently, fundamental analysis is a telescope, which allows seeing the whole picture, while technical analysis is a microscope that helps to understand the smallest details.

4. Following the latest news

First of all, pay attention to the latest information about the main macroeconomic indicators and news about particular coins. Macro statistics affect the volatility of financial instruments and the activity of traders around the world.

---

[8] Liquidity is about how big the trade-off is between the speed of the sale and the price it can be sold for. In a liquid market, the trade-off is mild: selling quickly will not reduce the price much.

I strongly recommend that you remember, or better, even write down a day of the week and the exact time when news reports on a particular coin are released to stay informed. To simplify news monitoring, I recommend creating a separate tab (page) with a calendar of statistics on your computer and viewing it from time to time.

5. Drawing up a trading plan

Although this section seems very simple, it is actually complicated as it's the most important aspect in the activity of every trader.

If you think that you can open a position after just scrolling down the news feed about a particular coin and making technical analysis of its chart, then God help you:-)

Of course, you may be lucky once, but in the long term, this method will result in permanent losses.

But what do I mean by drawing up a trading plan? A trading plan is a prearranged, detailed scenario of trader's actions in various market situations. That is, before you open a position, you determine the scenario of movement of a coin's price and the reaction of the bulk of traders. At the same time, we should not forget about the time when the news about a certain coin release. Thus, having viewed the calendar of events and understood which time the statistics are released, you get the time of the highest volatility. This time is best suited for the most risk-prone and morally sound traders. Therefore, I do not recommend sluggish traders being active 15 minutes before or after the news about a coin release.

Drawing up a trading plan and sticking to it is one of the main factors of your success. A disciplined approach is crucial!

6. Drawing up a risk management system and a money management system

A risk management system and a money management system are the most important components of each trader's activity. They secure approximately 20% of success in cryptocurrency trading.

The risk management system helps to organize trading in terms of risks. You can determine the scale of risks depending on different market situations.

The money management system, in turn, shows a trader how much money they should trade in a particular situation.

7. Understanding the psychology of trading participants

Although many traders miss this step, I view it as one of the most important prerequisites for successful trading. After all, psychology, namely the sense of the market and a traded coin, as well as understanding what the desires of traders at a given time are the lion's share of your profitable trades. In my opinion, about 70% of success accounts for psychology, 20% - the systems of risk management and money management, and only 10% - your trading strategy. Therefore, once again review your attitude towards the importance of understanding market participants' psychology.

8. Looking for entry points, planning stop loss and take profit placement

The fourth and fifth steps of our algorithm can brief you on an entry point. However, one should not treat the choice of such an important aspect too superficially. First, let's determine what the entry point is.

As you have already understood, this term means the moment of opening of a position (the direction and the ultimate goal do not matter).

You should be very responsible when choosing the entry point as the first step in trading has an impact on the final result and its size.

A stop-loss order is an order or price level of an instrument on the chart at which you close your position at a loss. In other words, you set the sum you are willing to risk in case of a price reversal.

A take-profit order specifies the exact price at which to close out an open position for a profit.

Remember that all these three aspects are critically important in trading!

So, you've got 8 steps of my personal trading algorithm, which you can upgrade for yourself. Do not try to follow it blindly. Instead, try to understand the basic principles of disciplined trading.

In the coming chapters, well look at each of these steps in greater detail. This is just the bird's-eye view.

Summary and Additional Considerations

First of all, assess your risks and the prospects of entry, i.e., you must understand the reasons for opening your position. I recommend that you write down when and at what price you open a position and at what price you will close it even before you open the position. Don't start to trade on a whim.

Early on, I advise you to use a daily chart for doing a technical analysis of the selected coin. Afterward, you can move to smaller timeframes, i.e., always move from bigger to smaller.

If you prefer trading altcoins, then no matter which one you choose, be sure to follow Bitcoin movements out of the corner of your eye. Whether you like it or not, Bitcoin remains to be a dominant coin. For example, according to the coinmarketcap.com, at the time of me writing the book, more than 54% of all the funds in the cryptocurrency market are concentrated in Bitcoin.

Bitcoin is an indicator of the entire cryptocurrency market, so I still recommend that you keep this coin in your portfolio.

As a bonus to the topic of developing a trading algorithm, I also want to share an idea of a table you can enter the data on all your coins in.

	A	B	C	D	E	F	G
1		% from deposit					
2			**Positions**				
3	BTC	5%	9234 (5%)	7820 (5%)			
4	BTG	20%	145,5 (10%)	110,3 (5%)	75 (5%)	51 (5%)	
5	XRP	20%	1,01 (5%)	0.938 (5%)	0,786 (5%)	0,686 (5%)	0,552 (5%)
6	ADA	20%	0,391 (5%)	0,359 (5%)	0,306 (5%)	0,2441 (5%)	0,1374 (5%)
7	XVG	10%	0,0510 (5%)	0,0462 (5%)	0,0384 (5%)		
8	USDT	20%					
9							
10			**Numerical values**				
11	BTC 8602 (5%) - bought (marked in green)						
12	BTC 7210 (5%) - quotes in market depth, pending execution (marked in black)						
13	XRP 1,01 (5%) - a coin bought at this price and listed for sale at a higher price (selling price indicated in Notes)						
14							
15							
16							
17							
18							

Link on the file: http://bit.ly/sample-portfolio

In the left corner of the table, we put down in a columnar form all the coins we have in our portfolio. Further, we denote their percentage in the portfolio. In the next column, we enter information about the price at which each coin was purchased. If coins were purchased at different prices, we designate each price in the following columns.

I also recommend that you divide all the figures in the table into three colors. I chose green, black and red. Green means that a coin is bought, black – it is put in a depth of market, i.e. is pending execution, which means these funds are blocked so far and you will be able to paint this figure green as soon as the purchase takes place. The red color means that a coin is bought at this price and is already listed for sale (we indicate the selling price in the Notes).

CHAPTER 4. TECHNICAL ANALYSIS

Successful cryptocurrency trading is impossible without the use of tools that estimate the behavior of the market. First, the cryptocurrency market has its regularities you should not ignore. Second, cryptocurrencies are very unstable, making intuitive forecasting more complicated. Technical analysis in cryptocurrency trading allows forecasting price fluctuations more successfully. So, if the fundamental analysis is about a coin value, technical analysis is about price.

What is technical analysis?

Technical analysis is a trading discipline employed to evaluate securities and identify trading opportunities by analyzing statistics gathered from trading activity, such as price movement and volume. Technical analysis allows determining what will happen to a certain currency price in the near future based on historical market data.

Japanese rice merchants started to use this method several centuries ago. Later, at the beginning of the 20th century, American journalist Charles Dow published a series of articles on finance, describing the patterns of growth and decline in the securities market. Later, the basic postulates were extracted from his works, forming the Dow Theory, which laid the cornerstone of technical analysis.

The Dow Theory created the practice of technical analysis and has made it possible to determine three basic theses of technical analysis. They are universal and applicable in the cryptocurrency market.

- *Nothing happens by accident.* Every price change in the market is caused by something. If you determine the cause, next time it will be easier to predict the movement of prices under similar circumstances.
- *History repeats.* What has already happened in the market can happen the second time. The consequences are likely to be the same.
- *Regularities work.* The trend (price movement vector) is likely to follow the same direction. Only a factor similar in strength can have an impact on it. Weaker factors lead to a temporary fluctuation (correction of cryptocurrency market), but not to a reverse trend.

Computers have made technical analysis much simpler as specialized charting software helps analyze price movements with different technical analysis tools: levels, lines, different indicators. Nowadays such charts are embedded in many cryptocurrency exchanges and work in an interactive mode.

Let's now analyze all the components of technical analysis in cryptocurrency trading. We will devote a separate section of the book to sort them out in detail. For now, I'll brief you on the basics of technical analysis for you to better understand the subsequent information.

So, apart from the price charts, the following components of the technical analysis are most well-known.

Levels. Support and resistance levels are most often used. These lines are drawn through the extreme points of a price movement chart. That is, through the high and low points. Why do we need them? First, history shows that we have an increased probability of an event at these levels. Second, by operating these levels skillfully, we understand there are certain *patterns* on the chart that also tend to produce particular outcomes.

Apart from patterns, we have more advanced tools for analysis called *indicators*. Thanks to specialized software, the data is processed on a chart to show you what is of practical value. But, as for me, not all indicators are of equal relevance. For example, *Japanese candlesticks* cannot give as much useful information as *Elliott waves* can.

The very first things the indicators analyze are candlesticks. Candlesticks show the open, close, maximum, and minimum prices for each period.

The second thing is the trade volume that shows the quantity of an asset which triggered a particular change and whether there was a trading activity within a certain candlestick or not.

A very important and convenient point is that traders can decide on their own what tools to choose for doing the technical analysis of a coin.

Having dealt with the components of technical analysis, I suggest considering its *advantages*:

- Initial data is accurate in the technical analysis
- Data is displayed in real time
- The technical analysis follows the same principle with all currencies
- Technical analysis provides sufficient data for trading little-known currencies.

Having highlighted the advantages, we should also point to the shortcomings of technical analysis:

- Late signals. For example, it's impossible to determine there will be growth on a certain week. You can be sure of this, say, the day before
- Inefficiency in case of interference of external factors. For example, you have made a forecast, everything goes according to a plan, but some news report on a coin is released and it crosses out your analysis. Unlike classical markets, it is a frequent phenomenon in the cryptocurrency market, not least because nobody is imprisoned for fiddling, therefore, unfortunately, a lot of market participants are playing a dirty game.

That's why technical analysis is less effective in the cryptocurrency market than in classical markets. Moreover, any technical analysis is a matter of interpretation. What does it mean? Nice charts with visible lines as shown in the books on trading (I do not mean mine:-) do not exist. Even the support and resistance levels can be drawn in different ways by different traders. The results of indicators can be interpreted in different ways too. Therefore, before making a decision on opening a position, a trader tries to find as many supporting factors as possible to justify the decision made. One of such factors is the results of computer analysis of the market.

So, the *computer analysis of the market* is the use and analysis of technical indicators. Technical indicators are mathematical calculations used to determine what may happen next with the price of a cryptocurrency.

There are several types of technical indicators:

- *Trend indicators* determine the likely direction of price movement. They are also called "lagging indicators." There are the following trend indicators: Moving Average, Bollinger Bands, Parabolic SAR, CCI and others
- *Oscillators* determine the likely point of price reversal. They are also called "leading indicators." There are the following types: RSI, MACD, Stochastic, Ichimoku, Momentum, and others
- *Volatility indicators* – indicators which assess the likely potential of a price
- *Non-price indicators* estimate non-price determinants of trade, such as volume, weighted volume, open interest, and

so on. There are the following types: OBV, Volumes, MFI, ZigZag, Alligator

- *Non-market indicators* which use values of price or volume for calculations (indicators of time, sequence, etc.)

Now let's consider one of the indicators, the Moving Average indicator, in practice. It has several types:

- MA is a simple moving average
- EMA - exponential moving average
- WMA - weighted moving average

So, if the moving average crosses the price chart and the price is at the top, it's a buy signal; if the price is below, it's a sell signal.

In turn, oscillators define overbought and oversold areas. An overbought/oversold area is the period of active redistribution of goods and funds between bulls and bears.

And here you have the final piece of information about the indicators to understand the overall picture of technical analysis. We will also examine them later in a separate section. There is such a notion as signals of divergence and convergence.

Divergence is a signal in the bull market, when the price peak on price chart makes a new high, while the price peak on the indicator makes a new low. This is a signal of a weakening trend.

Convergence is a signal in the bear market, when the price peak on price chart makes a new low, while the price peak on the indicator makes a new high. Convergence is a convergence of lines.

To open a position, I recommend that you use the data of technical indicators in conjunction with conducted complete technical analysis of the market.

Now, it's time to switch to the practical part of technical analysis. Get up the nerve, now a lot of charts will flash before your eyes. However, without them, it is impossible to make a qualitative forecast of the cryptocurrency price movement.

To start trading, you first need to learn trading slang. Now we will puzzle out a few words, while you can find a more extensive glossary of cryptocurrency terms at the end of this book.

Trading operations in the cryptocurrency market have nicknames: buy – go long; sell – go short. If you make a purchase, your operation is called a long position; if you sell something, the operation is called a short position.

Since the very foundation of all the financial markets (currency, stock, commodity, cryptocurrency markets), their participants, who make purchases are called "bulls", while those who sell assets are called "bears."

All analysts and speculators use various charts during the technical analysis as this is the simplest, most affordable and reliable way to compare prices over different time frames. After all, technical analysis is an exploration of price changes through the study of charts and with the aim of forecasting its further changes.

The most popular is the *Line Chart.*

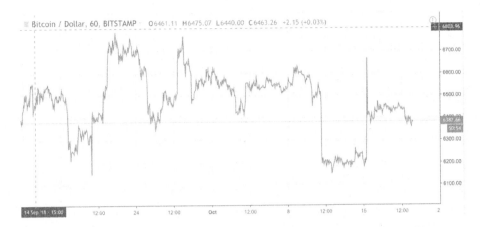

The line chart is the best to display price movement dynamics. A timeframe lies at the bottom of the chart, and the asset price scale is on the right.

Japanese candlesticks are the next most popular chart.

Here you need to distinguish between opening and closing prices of a candle as each candle is formed over a specific period.

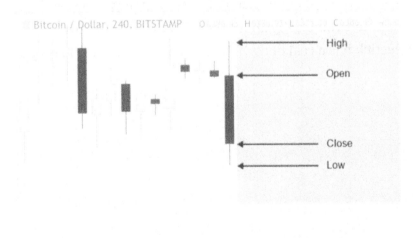

For example, a four-hour time frame is selected on this chart. Certain trading dynamics occur over this period of time. The previous candle closes in four hours, a new cycle comes and a new candle opens. If market participants begin to buy a coin during this period of time, then its price increases; if they take their profits (close the deal), the price falls. The more sellers are, the lower the price falls; the more buyers are, the higher the price rises. Therefore, we have a certain struggle between "bulls" and "bears": what color a candle will have because it can be red (color of "bears") or green (color of "bulls"). In the black and white book, these candles are black and white, respectively.

Now take a closer look at the chart on the previous picture. Do you notice something? No? What about some vertical formations? Such a formation is called a *shadow*. It shows the highest and the lowest traded price during the period of a candle formation.

We will devote a separate section to the Japanese candlesticks, but I want to tell you briefly about the candlestick structure. A candlestick has a real body (filled with color) and a shadow.

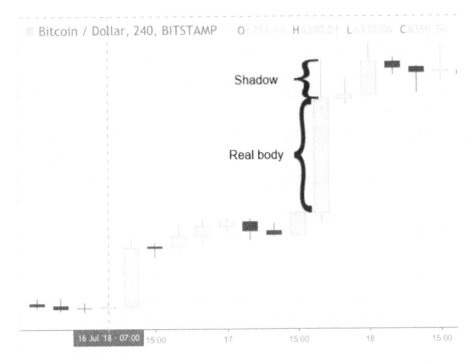

The next thing you need to remember in technical analysis is the timeframes within which a candle is being formed. I will list them on the table.

Chart	Timeframe
1M	1 minute
5M	5 minutes
30M	30 minutes
1H	1 hour
4H	4 hours
1D	1 day
1W	1 week
MN	1 month

You may use any timeframe for technical analysis, but keep in mind my recommendation: start with a larger time frame and gradually move to a smaller one.

And finally, memorize the main *laws of technical analysis*. As reminder, these are the three postulates of technical analysis. If the geometry is based on theorems, then the technical analysis is based on three postulates:

- Price takes into account everything
- Price movement is subjected to trends
- History repeats itself

Let's touch upon each postulate.

Price takes into account everything. For example, once some media reported that Ethereum co-founder Vitalik Buterin died. The price of ETH started to tumble. Later, Buterin denied this fake news by writing on the social network he was doing well. Right after that, the Ethereum price recovered. It is obvious that any news can provoke both decline and growth of a currency.

Price movement is subjected to trends. What is a trend? It is a directed movement. The trend can be ascending or descending. Accordingly, we tend to be up or down. There is no uncertain movement: either upward or downward. And any price movement depends on the direction of the trend that dominates in the market. If the trend is descending, the price will move down. If the trend is ascending, the price will move up. If the market is flat, the price will move horizontally.

History repeats itself. It does not matter how long the cryptocurrency market exists since its patterns, cycles and other components will always repeat themselves.

Apart from the main laws of technical analysis, there are also *laws of price movement*:

1. The current trend is more likely to last than to change direction.
2. The trend will develop in the same direction until it gives signs of a reversal.

Remember: *if you do not follow all these postulates, the market will "punish" you severely.*

CHAPTER 5. DRAWING SUPPORT AND RESISTANCE LEVELS

The basics of technical analysis deal with identifying and forecasting the trends on cryptocurrency charts. After determining the trend, we can proceed to graphical analysis (analysis of patterns) and computer analysis (analysis of indicators and oscillators data).

A trend is a direction in which the market moves. It is a series of zigzags that resemble a series of waves: rise is followed by fall.

There are three types of trends:

- Upward/bullish trend
- Downward/bearish trend
- Flat trend

To determine the current trend in the market, we need to look for the highest and the lowest prices of a coin on the chart.

For example, if we connect a large number of highest and lowest points with a line, we will see on this chart that the market is flat.

Now let's discuss each trend in more detail.

Upward/bullish trend

We need a chart to grasp the essence of this and other trends.

So, the chart shows different points, some of them are marked with the letter S, while some – with the letter P. What do they mean?

There is a simple formula for determining an upward trend. S1 and S2 are price peaks, while P1 and P2 are price bottoms. So, the essence of this formula is that P1 will always be less than P2, and S1 will always be less than S2. This means that at the upward trend each subsequent peak will be higher than the previous one, and each bottom will also be higher than the previous one.

Downward/bearish trend

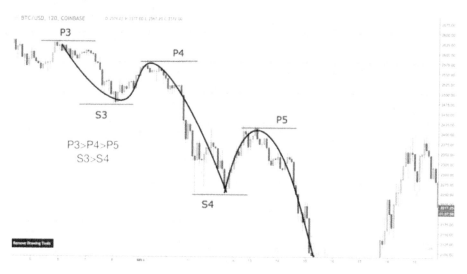

In case of a downward trend, P3 is more than P4 and more than P5. Each subsequent peak will be lower than the previous one, while each subsequent bottom will be lower than the previous one (S3 located higher than S4).

Flat trend

Here, F1, F2 and F3 are peak price points, and F4 and F5 are bottom price points. Both peak and bottom points stay on the same level. The price moves horizontally, like in a corridor, not updating the highs and lows. This indicates a flat market trend.

Thus, it is obvious that to start to do technical analysis, to determine the trend in the market, you only need to know the peak and bottom prices of a coin.

How to trade amid different trends? Of course, it is safer to trade when there is a bullish (upward) trend in the market. You can also trade amid a flat trend. A downward trend poses the biggest risk for your trading. Put simply, if the peaks and bottoms continue to be updated on the chart, there is no reason to worry. If peaks and bottom are not updated, it's a warning that a trend may reverse.

Support and resistance levels

We have already discussed what support and resistance levels are, so I suggest switching to practice immediately.

So, the bottom line on the chart is the support level, and the upper line is the resistance level. These levels help us to determine that this chart shows an upward trend.

Thus, it is obvious that a support level is a level below the market, where the desire to buy is so strong it can withstand the pressure of sellers. As a result, the fall is suspended and prices start to move up again. Usually, a support level can be determined in advance, according to the level of the previous decline. A resistance level, in turn, is the direct opposite of a support level and represents a level above the market, where the pressure of sellers exceeds the pressure of buyers.

The support and resistance levels can be of different strength. We need to learn how to pick out strong levels. **The first rule:** the longer the price hovers in the area of support or resistance, the more important this area is. For example, if the price was hovering near the support level for two weeks, and then went up, this area of support is more significant than if the same price fluctuations occurred for only two days.

The second rule: if the support level formation is accompanied by a large trade volume, this level is very significant. Conversely, the smaller the trade volume is, the less significant is the support level.

The third rule is determined by the remoteness of a support or resistance level in time from the present moment. Since we deal with the reaction of traders to the market movement and the positions, they either have already opened or not, it is clear that the closer the event is, the greater importance it gains as the market is activated to a greater extent.

How to draw a support level and a resistance level in Tradingview (a platform for technical analysis we have already discussed)?

We draw one level by linking the price peaks and bottoms. Afterward, to make the second level parallel to the first, we clone it and place prices on the other side of the price chart. To do this, click on the first drawn level and select "Clone" option in the taskbar. Thus, we get a level which is parallel to the one we drew before and now just move it to the area we need – the biggest number of points above or below the price chart.

Apart from these levels, many traders also draw horizontal lines on the chart. The principle of drawing is almost identical: we link the biggest number of points on one horizontal level with a line.

Trendline

A trendline is one of the simplest and clearest elements of technical analysis.

A trend line may be ascending and descending. We draw these lines the same way we draw support and resistance levels. The ascending line is drawn by connecting ascending lows, while the descending line is drawn by connecting descending highs. In order to verify the presence of a particular trend in the market, we need at least three points to draw a trend line. Once you find the third point on the chart and confirm the nature of the trend, you can use the trend line to solve a number of tasks.

For example, one of the fundamental principles of technical analysis is: a trend on the move will seek to continue its movement. Therefore, as soon as a trend gains pace and a trend line positions itself at a certain angle, this angle will usually remain unchanged in the course of further development of the trend. In this case, a trend line will allow us to determine the extreme points of the correction phases and also to indicate possible changes in the trend.

Suppose we have now an upward trend on our chart. In any case, corrective or intermediate price drops are inevitable on any chart. They, as a rule, will either approach an ascending trend line or touch it. When there is an upward trend, we expect to buy an asset at a low price. In this case, a trend line serves as a support level below the market. It's our buy zone. And vice versa: if our chart shows a downward trend, then we use a trend line as a resistance level for sale.

And as long as there are no breaks on the chart, a trend line helps us determine the buy and sell zones. But if a trend line breaks, it is the first sign of a change in the nature of the trend.

Technical line break

Do you notice something interesting in this chart?

I hope you've noticed the breakout through a resistance level. The price did not continue to move in the historical direction, updating the highs and lows, but "jumped" one level and went up. This happens when a closing price of the candlestick is fixed above the level.

What does this situation mean in the market? If we see a candle formation (especially its closing) behind a support or resistance level, this indicates a price reversal is looming. But if a candlestick, at first glance, makes its way beyond the level, but nevertheless closes below it, it's a "false breakout".

Acceleration of a trend

This chart shows an ascending trend, but a resistance level break occurred. We see here not a breakdown, which would signify a price reversal and change in trend, but a breakout. That is, the price breaks through a resistance level of ascending trend and continues to move upwards. Now our resistance level turns into the support level. Thus, the trend is accelerating.

If a trend is accelerating: the higher the degree of ascending trend is, the shorter in time this trend will last.

Drawing a channel

A channel is drawn almost automatically on your chart because you get it by drawing support and resistance levels. The area between these levels is called a channel.

A channel contains a channel line and a trend line. A trend line is the main one. If this line breaks on the chart, it means that the trend in the market has changed.

The main ascending trend line can be used for opening new positions. A channel line can serve as a guide for making profits in short-term operations. Some traders use a channel line to open short positions in the direction opposite to the main trend. However, it is very dangerous and, as a rule, unprofitable to trade against the market trend.

As in the case with the main trend line, the longer the channel lasts, the more important and reliable it becomes.

A main trend line break always indicates a change in trend. However, a break of channel's ascending line has the opposite meaning and means an acceleration of the existing trend. Many traders open additional positions after breakout amid upward trend.

I'll tell you a secret: in my opinion, building graphic patterns and channels is a very subjective concept. They are built with the help of inclined lines, and these lines can be drawn in different ways. For example, a trader may draw a line along either a body or a shadow of a candlestick, and the results will be different.

And now I'll cite an example of an interesting situation with building a channel on the chart. We had drawn a channel, but the situation in the market changed after a while and all our lines turned out to be below the price chart. What should we do?

The crossed area of the chart is the future we did not see when drawing a channel. In order to correct the situation and "return the chart in the channel" we have two options: change the angle of lines to capture the new highest point of the chart or expand the channel itself. We'll get the following result.

The first option is depicted with thick lines, the second one – with the thin ones.

Now I have a question for you: which of these two options is more correct? The answer is: both. The lines in both options help identify breakdown or breakout points, i.e., the zones where we receive a signal. So it does not matter how you draw the lines since if they show you the points of opening the position, your lines are drawn correctly.

To sum up, I want to say that such an analysis of a chart shows us the zones we need to monitor as we will open or close positions in these zones. However, this analysis does not show whether the price will break this zone or not.

Finally, write down and always remember the **golden rule of technical analysis**:

"Always conduct transaction following a dominant trend", i.e., if there is an upward trend in the market, you should buy; if there is a downward trend, you should sell.

Homework

1) Draw in Tradingview two examples of building a channel on 1h timeframe or higher
2) Draw two examples of building a channel on a timeframe lower than 1h

CHAPTER 6. GRAPHICAL ANALYSIS

We have studied the basic concepts of technical analysis in the previous section, and now I believe you are ready to move on to more complicated material – chart patterns.

All patterns of graphical analysis fall into two categories: reversal patterns and continuation patterns. Their names speak for themselves: reversal patterns indicate a break in the existing trend, while continuation patterns indicate a short pause after which a price movement will continue moving in the same direction.

At first glance, everything looks pretty simple, a kind of geometry on the chart: draw triangles and predict price movement. But in fact, creating valid chart patterns is much more complicated. The main point is the ability to distinguish between the patterns and not to be late to identify it in the process of formation. There are a lot of patterns in trading, but we will consider only a few of them.

I believe my main task as author and coacher is not to trouble you with many complicated words and concepts for boosting my profile, but to give you the knowledge necessary for trading. Therefore, I am sure that you will not need knowledge of dozens of chart patterns that fill other books on trading. The more patterns you know, the more you will be confused and it will be even harder for you to find them on the chart. You only need to know the most important ones that most often appear in the market.

Reversal patterns

Before we look at reversal patterns, let's grasp their general characteristics:

1. Prerequisite for the emergence of any reversal pattern is the existence of a previous trend
2. Warning about a possible reversal of existing trend may be a break of the important trend line
3. The larger the pattern (height and width) is, the more significant the subsequent market movement will be
4. Peak patterns are, as a rule, shorter in time and more variable than base patterns
5. Base patterns tend to have a smaller price range and more time is required to build them
6. A volume of trade often plays a more important role when a bearish-to-bullish reversal starts

Head and Shoulders pattern

Head and Shoulders (HaS) pattern is the main reversal pattern used in cryptocurrency as well as in other markets.

I depicted on the chart a classic example of a HaS.

This pattern forms only during the upward trend. The pattern was given its name for a real resemblance to the head and two shoulders of a man. The highest peak of the pattern is the head (it is in the middle), and the two smaller points are the left and the right shoulders (they are on both sides and about the same height). Formation of this pattern is considered complete when a closing price of a candlestick is fixed below the neckline (the neckline is depicted with the horizontal level, which passes through the last two lows and is a support level).

This means that the market, having broken a trend line, descends below the support level and heads towards a downward trend. If HaS pattern is confirmed with volumes, it's time for us to close long (buy) positions. However, if any pattern is formed without significant volume, the probability it will not hit the target on the chart (the price will move not according to the predicted direction) ramps up.

Now I want to reveal a secret: there are no ideal patterns on a live chart. All patterns tend to be crooked, but readers are usually not warned about it. That's why, having studied up a couple of manuals on trading for dummies, you still can find practically no pattern that looks like what you saw in the book, because the real world doesn't correspond to textbook theories.

Therefore, I prefer showing you the patterns on real charts. Subsequently, I want to warn you are unlikely to meet a HaS pattern in its most ideal manifestation on the chart. As a rule, the shoulders may not be equal, and the neckline may be inclined.

But the key question remains open: if we see a HaS pattern on the chart, how can we understand how far the market will go down after it is completed? It's simple! We measure the distance from the head to the neckline and put this height down from the neckline break.

To this end, Tradingview has a special tool called "Price range". For example, the height of the Head and Shoulders pattern is 10%. What does this figure mean? It shows how far the market will "slope" in the near future. In this case, we are talking about a reversal of an upward trend, so the market will go down by 10%.

And *here is one of my top-secret tips*:

Never use the exact height of the pattern for the forecast, it's better to take 70% of this pattern. So, if the height of the pattern is 10%, we aim at 7% of a reversal from the original height. 7% is our target for profit taking.

One more nuance concerns the measurement of the height of a pattern: whether we should measure it from the highest point of a real body or from the highest point of an upper shadow. If the shadows are not sky-high, I mean they do not exceed the height of candlestick several times, we should measure from the highest point of upper shadows. If they are too high, then we do not take them into account.

Inverse Head and Shoulders

This reversal pattern forms on the chart only during a downward trend. It is a mirror reflection of the Head and Shoulders patterns. It also has a head, a left, and a right shoulder, but they are arranged upside down.

The height of this pattern is also measured from the neckline level to the highest point at the top of the head.

Double Top

This trend reversal pattern occurs on the chart often. A double top is, perhaps, the most wide-spread pattern after the Head and Shoulders. It forms only during the uptrend. The pattern is characterized by two consecutive peaks in price located on one horizontal level.

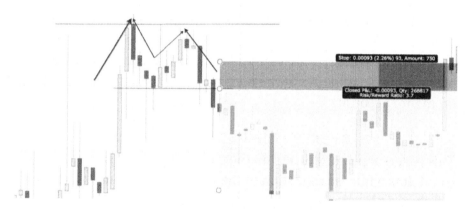

As we can see on the left side of the chart, this pattern has two peaks and they are on the same level. It is considered that the pattern has completed its formation when the closing prices overcome the level of decline (the neckline level in HaS pattern). As a rule, the formation of the second peak is accompanied by a smaller trade volume, but the volume increases at the breakdown. This testifies to a change in trend when the growth phase is followed by the decline phase. The minimum level to which the price will drop after the breakdown is also determined on the basis of its height. To do this, we measure the distance from the pattern's peak to its support level and then lay off this height from

104

the breakpoint downward. The target of the Double Top pattern is shown on the right side of the chart.

Double Bottom

This pattern is a mirror reflection of the Double Top pattern. While Double Top forms during the uptrend, Double Bottom forms during the downtrend. The first figure looks like the letter "M", while the second resembles the letter "W."

This pattern can give a lot of false signals. Therefore, determine the strength of this pattern before placing the orders. Here, trade volume is also important when the price breaks out. If the trade volume increases along with the formation of the second peak, this indicates a true reversal of the downward trend.

The chart shows there was a downtrend in the market but it reversed after the formation of the Double Bottom pattern. For subsequent forecasting of the price, we also measure the height of the pattern and get the percentage of its target. It will tell us the price range for profit taking.

Triple Top

The difference in this pattern from the Double Top is that it has three peaks, not two. It also very much resembles the Head and Shoulders pattern but unlike the HaS, all three its price peaks are on the same level. Each of the three peaks should be accompanied by a decrease in the trade volume. The pattern is considered to be completed when prices overcome the level of decline with a cocurrent increase in volume. To get price forecasts, we also measure the height of this pattern (from peak to support level) and then lay off the obtained value from the breakpoint downward.

Triple Bottom

This pattern is a mirror reflection of the Triple Top pattern with the only difference that volume, as a confirming factor, is more important when price breaks out.

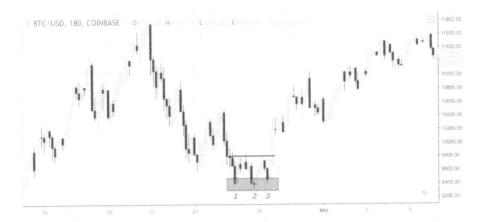

The Triple Bottom pattern is considered reliable in trading. However, it takes a long time to form, so often a trader runs out of patience before it is formed. All three price lows of this pattern are equal, and their formation sometimes takes several months. Therefore, if you want to see this pattern, look for coins with a long downward trend.

We have completed the review of patterns. I want to note that you do not need to remember the names of all these patterns. The main thing is to try to understand where the trend may reverse. To do this, monitor the update of price highs and lows. After all, as soon as the lows and highs are not changing, a pattern starts to appear on the chart.

Trend continuation patterns

Now we proceed to the *trend continuation patterns*.

These patterns are more short-dated and tell us not about a trend break but show a small period of consolidation or a pause, after which the price will continue to move in the same direction, i.e., the trend will not change.

Triangle

The first pattern we will pay special attention to in this category is, of course, a triangle. Every trader in every market is familiar with this pattern. It is a basic one for technical analysis, and, perhaps, is the most often-observed on the charts. I want to mention that all triangles are classified as trend continuation patterns, but personally, I consider them to be "non-trend patterns" or "patterns of uncertainty."

I imagine you're raising your eyebrows in surprise. I'll explain.

In the process of their formation in the market, triangles accumulate volume and volatility, forming a kind of spring. At the beginning of this pattern, we see the main impulse on the chart, after which volatility begins to decrease. Sooner or later one of the levels on the chart - resistance or support - will be breached by a pattern. Therefore, personally, I view a triangle as an uncertain pattern because after a pattern is formed, the price may either continue the existing trend or reverse the market.

There are three types of triangles:

- Symmetrical
- Ascending
- Descending

All these triangles are different in shape and, consequently, point to different market movements. Let's take a closer look at each of them.

Symmetrical Triangle

It is the most often-observed type of triangle in the market. It consists of two converging trend lines with a price sandwiched between them. The upper line of the pattern falls and the lower line rises. The pattern is considered complete when the closing price is fixed outside of either of the two lines.

To measure a symmetrical triangle, take the height of its base and lay it vertically off from the breakpoint of the pattern.

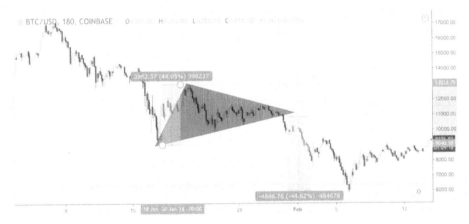

It is the symmetrical triangle which I consider to be the most insidious as it is difficult to determine whether the price will go up or down after breaking this pattern. To make my forecasts more accurate, I, as in all other cases, use volume. If the upward movement of the price is accompanied by an increase in volume, I predict breakout. And vice versa, if the downward price movement is accompanied by an increase in volume, the breakdown is most likely to happen. However, non-standard situations also happen.

For example, your symmetrical triangle breaches the upper trendline, making you buy coins, but then the spring went back into a triangle, formed a peak and started to fall rapidly. What happened? The upper zone of the triangle was adjusted, so what you called a breach was false breakout. The thing is we do not have a clear level a price may cross; we have a spring, the higher and lower points of which may be adjusted. Therefore, in our example, the price reversed and ran down to the height of the triangle. If you do not close the position on time, you lose money.

Ascending triangle

Ascending triangle (as well as a descending triangle) is considered to be a type of symmetrical triangle. But all of them differ significantly. Ascending triangle is considered to be a bullish pattern, descending triangle - bearish, while the symmetrical triangle is believed to be neutral.

The ascending triangle is formed on an uptrend. As a rule, this pattern is formed near a strong resistance level, predicting its breakout. In this triangle, the price is squeezed between the horizontal upper trend line (resistance level) and the lower trend line rising diagonally.

The ascending triangle is considered to be formed when the price closes beyond the resistance level. We measure the height of the triangle's base and lay it off from the breakout point. But do not forget that a breakout must be accompanied by a sharp increase in volume. With subsequent price drops, the upper resistance level should turn into a support level.

Descending Triangle

Unlike the previous pattern, the descending triangle is formed on a downtrend near a strong support level. This pattern has a horizontal lower trend line, while the upper trend line declines diagonally.

The formation of this pattern is completed with a breakdown at the lower horizontal line. To measure a figure, it is necessary to take the height of triangle's base and then lay it off from the breakdown point downwards.

On this chart, the descending triangle has hit a target as a trend continuation pattern. However, although the descending triangle usually forms during a downtrend, it also sometimes occurs at the top of the market.

We have considered all types of triangles, each of which has its own features, but there are a number of points typical of all triangles without exception:

1. There must be at least five waves in a classical triangle. If a triangle breaks the level before all the waves are formed, the price is unlikely to have enough force to move in a certain direction
2. Trade volume and the price inside the pattern may help predict a break in a triangle. For example, if the price inside the triangle has reversed before reaching one of the trendlines, the price is likely to break the opposite trendline as soon as it reaches it
3. If you trade manually, then place a market order when a candlestick, which broke the triangle's trendline, closes beyond its limits.

Flag

This pattern marks a short pause in the existing trend. The flag pattern may form during both upward and downward trends. As a rule, the formation of this pattern is preceded by a steep and almost straight line of price movement. The market seems to rush way ahead of itself and therefore, it should have a rest for a while. After that, the price will continue its movement in the same direction.

The flag pattern forms between two parallel trend lines that tend to slope against the prevailing trend. During the uptrend, the flag moves downwards; during the downtrend, it moves upwards. After this pattern is formed, the price should cover in the same direction the distance equal to the height of the pattern's flagpole.

To confirm the flag pattern formation, I use the same time-honored volume. It should grow during the expected break.

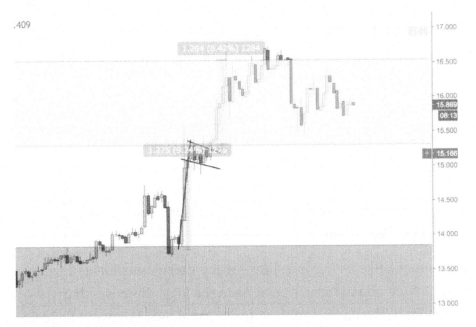

What do we see on this chart? We observe the directional movement of the market - a flagpole - as a sharp impulse, followed by a small horizontal price movement. How do we predict the market movement during this pattern? We measure the height of a flagpole and lay off 70% of this height upwards. Why upwards? Because the flag is a trend continuation pattern, and our chart depicts uptrend.

I will also reveal my personal observation regarding this pattern.

If after two flags in a row you notice the immediate formation of the third one on the chart (and you can see this often enough), be aware that the third flag is always false.

That is if a flag has formed on your chart, hit the target (so we got the second flag), but afterward we see the formation of the third flag, we must understand that it is false, and, therefore, it will not reach the target.

Pennant

This pattern (like Flag) is among the most reliable trend continuation patterns. The Pennant consists of a flagpole and two converging trend lines. The pattern resembles a small Symmetrical Triangle, which stands on a flagpole and forms amid a gradual significant reduction in trade volume.

A Pennant, like a Flag, is a short-term pattern as its formation takes from one to three weeks. As in the Flag, there is a sharp impulse in the Pennant at first (price hike). It is the way a flagpole of the pattern is formed. Then there is a pause, followed by the continuation of a price movement. The pattern is considered to be formed when the price breaks the top trend line during an uptrend and the lower trend line during a downward trend.

We should confirm the genuineness of this pattern (as in the case of all other patterns) with the trade volume, which should increase during a break. But remember that increase in volume is more important to confirm the breakout rather than breakdown.

Wedge

This pattern is often confused with triangle and pennant, so let me explain the differences between them.

Unlike Triangle, both trend lines of the Wedge pattern are directed horizontally either up or down. Wedge is more elongated in the direction of movement, either up or down, and the Triangle is stretched wide. As for Pennant, it has a flagpole on which consolidation takes place. If you add a flagpole to Wedge pattern, it will turn into Pennant pattern.

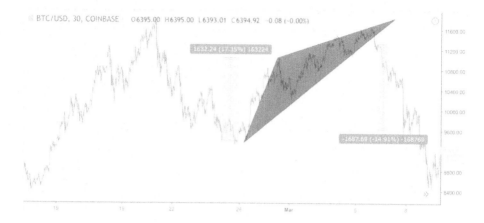

Wedges can signal either bullish or bearish price reversals, i.e., they can form both during upward and downward trends.

In fact, there are many more other graphic patterns in technical analysis, for example, Saucer, Cup with Handle, Diamond, etc. But they appear on charts so rarely that I decided not to focus on them in this book.

All the patterns can be analyzed on different time frames, but always check yourself in smaller intervals. So, if you see a beautifully formed triangle on 4-hour though it is absent on a 1-hour scale, do not hurry to make forecasts.

In general, a chart of every cryptocurrency (especially Bitcoin) is crowded with various patterns. You just need to learn to distinguish them and draw correctly. This will come with practice. Draw the patterns in Tradingview, then delete them and start all over again. You will get the hang of it with repetition

Homework

1) Draw in Tradingview two examples of triangles indicating the level of the break, entry point, and target
2) Draw two examples of reversal patterns indicating the level of the break, entry point, and target
3) Draw two examples of trend continuation patterns indicating the level of the break, entry point, and target

CHAPTER 7. COMPUTER ANALYSIS

Technical analysis in trading is not only about support and resistance levels, trend lines, channels, and patterns. It also covers mathematical methods that we use to build indicators, which, in turn, act as filters for determining the market properties. It is a sort of mathematical calculation: "This is how the price behaves."

Technical indicators help traders not to tie themselves into knots over the informational flow of the price chart. They systematize all the data and hint whether the market is overbought or oversold now, whether we should open or close a position.

In other words, if you do not use any indicator during technical analysis, you are a strange trader. After all, indicators are not only additional tools in the pile of your trading terminology, they simplify your life significantly. Each indicator was developed by someone who mathematically transformed the price stream in such a way that it would be easier for you to analyze a chart and make correct trading decisions.

However, it's not all as easy as it sounds. The signals of indicators often turn out to be false. Then how can we trust them? Do not focus on one indicator and always confirm the signal of one indicator with others. For example, if the moving average tells you now it is the best time for selling, do not rush, wait for the corresponding confirmation from the oscillators (a kind of indicators, which we'll discuss later).

Choosing the right indicator is also important. Different indicators may be suitable for each market and even each traded instrument (in our case, cryptocurrency). The indicators work differently on different timeframes. For example, if a certain indicator generates signals well on the D1 chart, it will lie through the teeth on 1H. There are leading and confirming indicators. Leading indicators get ahead of the price chart and signals in advance to buy or sell while confirming indicators just confirm the current market trend.

Therefore, my friends, do not ask me which indicator works best. Test different indicators with different currencies and on different timeframes by trial and error method.

All technical indicators are divided into three types:

- Trend indicators (SMA, EMA, WMA, Ichimoku Cloud, etc.) which identify the likely price direction, i.e., the presence of a particular trend
- Oscillators (RSI, MACD, Stochastics, etc.) which identify the likely point of price chart reversal (they may be trend and flat), define overbought and oversold zones, helping to decide when to open the position
- Volume indicators which identify the market volume at a certain point of time

Trend indicators

All trend indicators are designed to identify the condition of the market. They:

- Determine the presence and direction of the trend
- Generate trading signals
- Are used as dynamic support and resistance levels

Despite the benefits of these indicators, do not forget that they are lagging a bit, so when you receive a signal from the trend indicator, wait for the confirmation from the oscillator.

And now let's delve into the most popular trend indicators.

Moving Average

Simple Moving Average (SMA) is the most common trend indicator. It gives an average price of a traded instrument over a particular time period and identifies the main trend. It looks like a smooth line on the chart.

A simple or arithmetic moving average is calculated by adding recent closing prices of a traded instrument over a certain number of time periods (for example, 12 hours) and then dividing that sum by the number of time periods. The formula is the following:

SMA = SUM (close(i), N/N, where *SUM* is the sum, *close (i)* is the closing price of the current time period, *N* is the number of calculation periods.

For example, we have 12 candlesticks. We add all the closing prices of these 12 candlesticks and divide by 12. Thus, we average the price on the chart, at each point in which the price will be presented for a certain period of time. This time interval is called the moving average period.

All the moving averages are lagging because we average the price. If the price on your chart goes up or down sharply, this indicator will react but you will receive this signal with a delay.

There are three main types of moving averages:

- SMA (Simple moving average)
- EMA (Exponential moving average)
- WMA (Weighted moving average)

What do they differ from each other?

Simple moving average applies equal weight to all data points.

Exponential moving average places a greater weight and significance on the most recent data points. This means it places significance starting from the last bar.

Weighted moving average. While the significance of bars decreases more smoothly in exponential moving average, the importance of bars decreases in a more pronounced manner in weighted moving average as it gives importance to different bars.

What is the most popular trading strategy using the moving average?

When the price crosses above the moving average, it's a buy signal. When it crosses below, it's a sell signal. So we buy, when the closing price is above MA; and we sell, when the closing price is below MA.

On the Tradingview platform, you can find the moving average (as well as all other indicators) in the "Indicators" section on the upper taskbar.

If you want to resort to help of a moving average during trading, then you need to learn how to choose the right time period, which will generate a minimum of false signals. It's a matter of practice.

And now let's consider an example of moving averages on the chart.

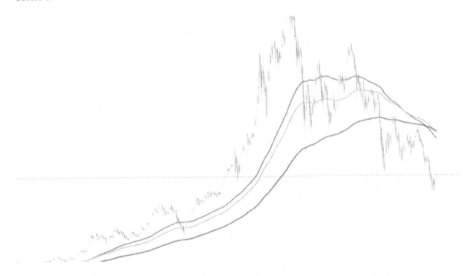

The lowest line on this chart is a simple moving average, the middle line is an exponential moving average, and the top line is a weighted moving average.

All types of moving averages can be used on different time frames. It depends on your trading strategy and whether you are a long-term investor or a scalp trader.

Ichimoku Cloud

The Ichimoku Kinko Hyo (Ichimoku Cloud) technical indicator developed back in the 1930s by Japanese analyst Goichi Hosoda, who used the pseudonym Ichimoku Sanjin. He invented this indicator for predicting the movement of Japan Nikkei stock index. The analyst improved his indicator for more than thirty years and made the results public in the 1960s.

The Ichimoku Cloud includes 5 lines, resembling moving averages, with exotic names:

1. Tenkan-sen (so-called "Conversion Line"; It's the midpoint of the 9-day high-low range)
2. Kijun-sen (differs from Tenkan-sen by the value of the time interval)
3. Senkou Span A (it's the midpoint of Tenkan-sen and Kijun-sen lines)
4. Senkou Span B (another moving average with an even longer period)
5. Chikou Span (built from closing prices).

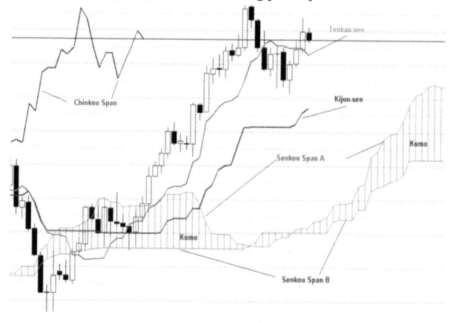

When intersecting, these 5 lines form a kind of zone we call "cloud." The clouds are of two kinds: red and blue. Red clouds are formed when Senkou Span A line is above Senkou Span B line. Blue clouds are formed when Senkou Span B line is above Senkou Span A line.

The Ichimoku indicator is a complex tool and combines several market analysis strategies. It is designed to identify trends, support and resistance levels and generate buy or sell signals.

So how does the Ichimoku indicator generate signals for traders?

1. A signal of three lines (three lines are built according to volatility, from the most volatile to the least volatile, i.e., from the short-term trend to the long-term trend. If they line up from top to bottom, we have an uptrend; if bottom to top - a downtrend)

2. A signal of crossing the lines (if Tenkan-sen crosses Kijun-sen from bottom to top, it's a buy signal; if Tenkan-sen crosses Kijun-sen from top to bottom, it's a sell signal)

3. Signal formed by a combination of indicator lines and price chart (remember that since the indicator lines average the price, they are less volatile than the price chart, and therefore the price chart will generate signals)

4. Chikou Span signal (if this line crosses the chart from bottom to top, it's a buy signal; if it crosses from top to bottom, it's a sell signal)

5. A signal of indicator clouds (if the price is above the clouds, we have an upward trend; if the price is below the clouds, we have a

downward trend; while the price in the cloud itself indicates the flat market).

Let's now consider an example of a signal generated by Ichimoku indicator.

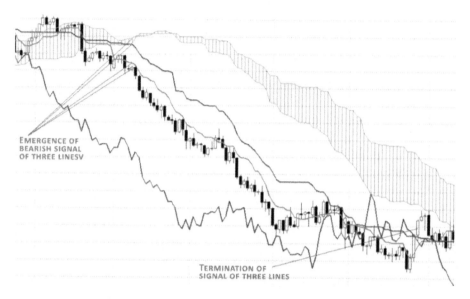

EMERGENCE OF
BEARISH SIGNAL
OF THREE LINESV

TERMINATION OF
SIGNAL OF THREE LINES

This chart shows a bearish signal. The price crosses the indicator lines from top to bottom, so we get a sell signal. In case you speculate for fall, you can hold a short position until the price does not cross, for example, Kijun-sen line. Close the position when the price crosses the same line in the opposite direction.

This chart shows three lines of the indicator, which serve as additional support and resistance levels. With the help of the cloud we can also determine we have an upward trend, so once we notice that the lines form up in the correct order (that is, as their volatility decreases), we understand we can add positions when bouncing off these levels.

On the top of the chart we see the intersection of the cloud, which indicates that the trend ends, so we need to close the positions.

What's good about Ichimoku indicator? If a moving average takes the closing prices of candlesticks for a certain period of time and divides, for example, by 5, the Ichimoku indicator is built on high and low prices, i.e., it takes the entire candlestick along with its shadows.

For example, as we have already said, Tenkan-sen line is built as a midpoint of the 9-day high-low range. The formula is as follows (H9 + L9) / 2. This line defines a short-term trend.

If the situation in the market changes dramatically, the Tenkan-sen line will react to it since it takes into account the entire candlestick with shadows, not only the closing price. This distinguishes the line of this indicator from a simple moving average, which always lags. This makes Ichimoku indicator unique: it does not average the price, but takes all the market volatility and gives us an assessment of the current situation.

Finally, I want to note that although the Ichimoku Cloud indicator is a powerful tool for a trader, you should not consider it as a panacea. Use it in conjunction with other indicators and oscillators.

Alligator

Despite its terrible name, the Alligator indicator is popular among traders around the world. It was developed by Bill Williams, a pioneer of chaos theory.

This indicator is a usual combination of three smoothed moving averages (SMMA - Smoothed Moving Average) set at 13, 8, 5 periods and shifted by 8, 5 and 3 bars respectively.

The three moving averages have their name:

- Jaw of the Alligator
- Teeth of the Alligator
- Lips of the Alligator

1 - JAW OF THE ALLIGATOR
2 - TEETH OF THE ALLIGATOR
3 - LIPS OF THE ALLIGATOR

Which one do you think is the most volatile? The right answer is Lips. Lips of the Alligator will generate the biggest number of signals. How to determine the most volatile line? It's very simple. This line is the closest one to the price. The Lips of the Alligator (3rd line) start with the five-bar SMMA; the Teeth of the Alligator (2nd line) start with the eight-bar SMMA; and the Jaw of the Alligator (1st line) starts with the 13-bar SMMA.

When the three lines are criss crossing each other, the **alligator is sleeping** at this time. And the longer the dream lasts, the hungrier it becomes. If to speak a mathematical language, the long-term crisscrossing of moving averages is the usual consolidation of prices.

After the Alligator gets enough sleep, "interesting" things begin to happen. The first thing it does after it wakes up is to open its mouth and **yawn**. Then he smells prey (a bear or a bull) and starts to hunt it. Having eaten enough, the Alligator loses the interest in food so the indicator lines crisscross again (it's time to take profit). From the point of view of technical analysis, it's a usual break of a trading range, the strength of which depends on the duration of consolidation.

When all the Alligator lines join together - we have a flat. As soon as the lines move apart (Alligator wakes up), we should open position.

This indicator works very poetically. However, I have one remark: the Alligator indicator is technical on volatile, high-volume coins. If you open the chart of any shitcoin and try to apply this indicator, it will not generate signals.

Oscillators

As I have already explained, the oscillator is a type of indicator. However, unlike trend indicators, oscillators can be used not only during an upward or downward trend but during flat markets as well. Each oscillator indicates overbought and oversold zones on the price chart.

Oscillators are leading indicators, which means that a trader receives a buy or a sell signal even before it is visible on the chart.

Moreover, the oscillators demonstrate convergence and divergence (convergence and divergence of the indicator chart with the price chart).

Oscillators have gained popularity among traders due to the simplicity of their creation and use.

RSI

Relative strength index (RSI) is perhaps the most popular oscillator. It was developed by American engineer Welles Wilder in 1978.

RSI is a wide-spread and useful technical indicator that shows how much the price is changing in the direction of its movement. It transforms the price into the percent, thereby indicating overbought zones (below 30%) and oversold zones (above 70%).

Thus, RSI values of 30% or below are interpreted as indicating an oversold condition, while RSI values of 70% or above indicate that security is becoming overbought. When the price from the overbought zone enters the neutral zone, it is a sell signal; when the price from the oversold zone enters the neutral zone, it's a buy signal.

Here is a list of signals this oscillator generates:

- Overbought/oversold zone: when the RSI oscillator value is closer to 100% or 0%, respectively
- Divergence: when the indicator chart forms extremes in the direction opposite to the direction of price movement
- The trend on the indicator usually coincides with the trend on the price chart up to any of the cases above

The convergence or divergence of price and indicator charts is one method for determining the termination of the trend in the market. Usually, after such signals, the price goes in the direction of the oscillator.

CCI

Commodity channel index (CCI) is a technical indicator based on an analysis of the current change in price deviation from its average value for a certain period and the average statistical value of this parameter.

This oscillator, like the RSI, indicates overbought and oversold zones in the market. You can use it in several strategies. A classic strategy is when deals occur when CCI rises above 100% or drops below 100%. This means:

For long positions:

- buy when CCI rises above + 100%
- sell when CCI drops below + 100%

For short positions:

- sell when CCI drops below -100%
- buy when CCI rises above -100%

Some traders recommend using a zero value as a signal line, calling this strategy a Zero CCI indicator:

- Buy (open a long position, close short position) when CCI rises above 0
- Sell (close long position, open short position) when CCI drops below 0

Now let's consider an example.

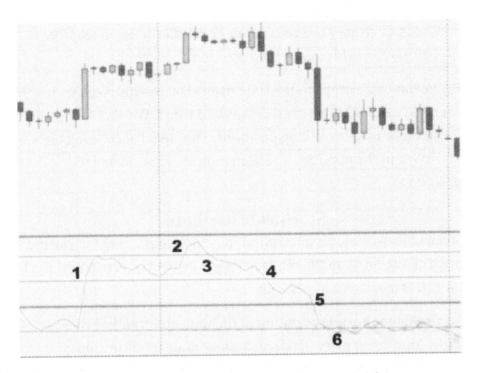

1. CCI indicator is located in the overbought zone, i.e., between +100 and +200. It's a sign of a strong uptrend - a buy signal.

2. Being above +200 in the overbought zone, you can mark an early trend reversal. Here you should set a stop-loss or close position, based on the behavior of candlesticks. As an option, you may wait for the indicator to cross +200 in the opposite direction.

3. CCI, having dropped from the overbought zone, is in the range of +200 - +100. It is worth closing long transactions and preparing for the opening of positions for sale.

4. CCI curve moved to the range of +100 - 0, the price left the overbought zone. Close long positions, open short positions.

5. When CCI crosses the zero boundary and is in the range from 0 to -100, you should open selling positions.

6. The indicator drops to the zone from -100 to -200, i.e., the oversold zone. We observe a downward trend. We should increase the number of short-selling positions. The signal of crossing the -100 mark in the opposite direction indicates the closing of position.

Stochastic oscillator

Stochastic oscillator is a technical indicator comparing the closing price of a security to the range of its prices over a certain period of time. It is measured in percent.

According to the interpretation of the indicator's author George Lane, the closing price of the next time frame tends to stop near previous highs during uptrend; and the closing price of the next time frame tends to stop near previous lows during a downtrend. Thus, a stochastic oscillator presents the location of the closing price of a stock in relation to the high and low range of the price of a stock over a period of time.

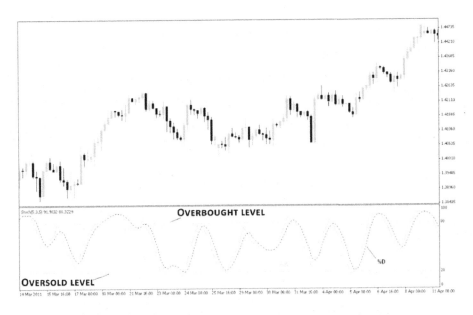

The stochastic oscillator has two more lines (apart from overbought and oversold zones) inside, which work after the manner of moving averages. They crisscross and generate signals.

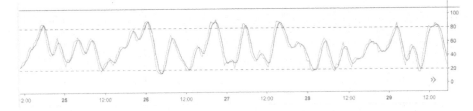

How to trade using the stochastic indicator?

- Buy when oscillator leaves oversold zone (above 20%), and sell when oscillator leaves overbought zone (below 80%)
- Buy when the fast line (%K) crosses a slow line (%D) from bottom to up; sell during the opposite movement
- Identify divergences, i.e., discrepancies between oscillator and price chart.

Personally, I use stochastic indicator (and all other oscillators in general) not to identify overbought and oversold zones, but to find divergence and convergence. To indicate them, I use, for example, CCI and RSI, while bundled with the stochastic indicator I see the price reversal on the chart.

MACD

Moving average convergence divergence indicator (MACD) is a technical indicator developed by Gerald Appel. The indicator is used to check the strength and direction of the trend and to indicate reversal points. It consists of two moving averages with different time periods.

There are two options for building MACD indicator: linear and histogram. The linear indicator has the form of two moving averages (fast and slow), while the histogram has columns that show the distance between these lines.

It is also possible to identify divergence and convergence, using this indicator.

I have a question for you. Which line on this chart generates signals better?

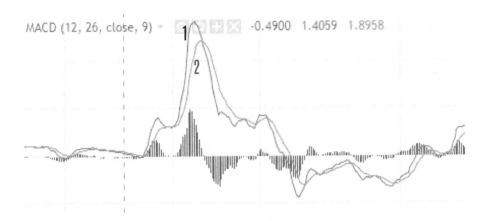

MACD (12, 26, close, 9) -0.4900 1.4059 1.8958

I have a question for you. Which line on this chart generates signals better? I hope you answered "the 1st line", because it is the correct answer.

Crossing the signal line from bottom to top is a buy signal; from top to bottom is a sell signal. As for the histogram: when it goes from a negative zone to positive, it's a buy signal; when it moves from positive to negative, it's a sell signal. In this case, the higher the bars are, the stronger is a bullish trend; the lower the bars are, the stronger is a bearish trend.

And remember: this oscillator works best on the flat market and on large timeframes.

Divergence and convergence

We have already mentioned that divergence is a discrepancy between the values of price chart and indicator. Convergence is jst the opposite term when the values of price chart and indicator approach each other. But despite their differences, both these phenomena are called divergence in technical analysis.

It is the divergence that is considered one of the most reliable and strong signals in technical analysis. But do not forget that you cannot rely on only one indicator. Although I know a large number of professional traders who make market forecasts and trade using only divergence.

So, there can be a bullish or a bearish divergence in the market. If the higher high on the chart is not confirmed by high on the oscillator, then we are talking about a bearish divergence. If the lower low on the chart is not supported by low on the oscillator, we have a bullish divergence.

As a rule, divergence signals to a weakening of the existing trend and possible strong correction or reversal. The larger the timeframe is, the stronger is the signal.

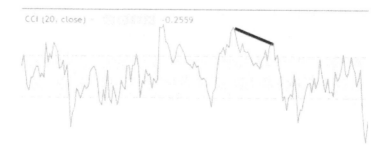

CCI (20, close) · 0.2559

In other words, the divergence is when the highest points on the chart go up, and on the oscillators, they go down. It is a signal that the price will move in the direction indicated by the oscillator. This signal can be considered reliable as it hit the target in 80% of cases.

To confirm the divergence in the price chart, at least two oscillators are needed. For example, if you use three oscillators and only one of them shows divergence – it is a false signal. You need positive data from two oscillators, but it's better when all three oscillators show the same signal. A stronger divergence should be considered on large timeframes.

Convergence is approximation between price chart and oscillator, implying manifestation of the same signs. Convergence is the process which is opposite to divergence.

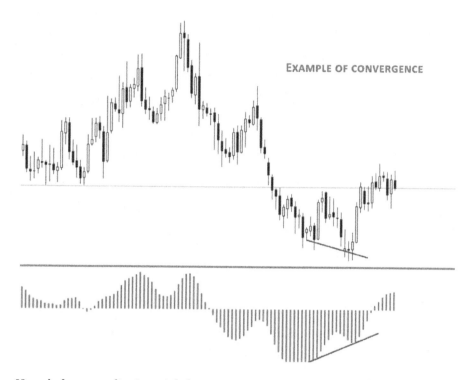

EXAMPLE OF CONVERGENCE

Here's how to distinguish between strong, medium and weak divergence and convergence. I recommend that you keep this "cheat sheet" for yourself.

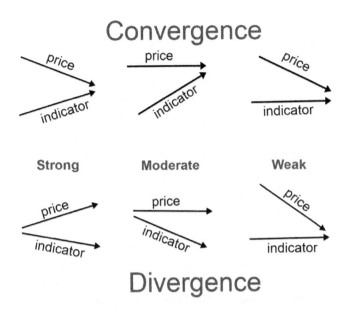

Here is an example of divergence and convergence on a live chart.

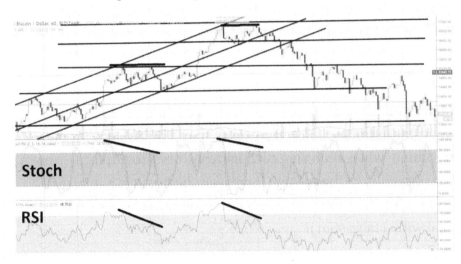

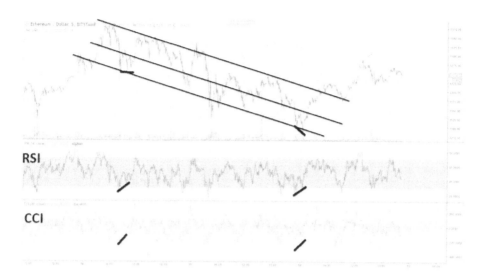

Volume

This indicator is usually built under the price chart and shows the volume of trade (sale and buy transactions) over a certain period of time. Indicator "Volume", unlike its previous "colleagues," does not generate buy or sell signals. It works as an auxiliary tool, helping to determine the strength of a particular trend. The larger volume confirms a particular trend, the more chances to hit the target it has.

I hope you remember that we have already discussed this indicator in the sections on patterns since I always pay attention to volume when analyzing each pattern. It is also important for break validity. If the volume increases, the break is not false. If there is a sharp spike in price but the volume remains small, we deal with a false signal.

Basically, this indicator demonstrates the interest of market participants in a particular price movement. The more people who open positions when the price moves in one or another direction, the more likely the continuation of this movement and the greater is the volume indicator.

Here I want to make a small remark. Personally, I believe that the volume is a very controversial indicator, as it can be "drawn" artificially on a chart. But who can do this and how? Of course, the major market players with large capital can do this. One player can buy a large amount of currency, thus creating a semblance of consumer interest in the market. The same can be done by selling a large amount of currency, imitating the desire of all market participants to "get rid" of this currency. Therefore, be sure to pay attention to the volume when trading this or that cryptocurrency. If you notice that the market is growing, but the volume remains the same, just ask yourself: Why do the large players "draw" the volume now?

Homework

1) Make two forecasts on entry and exit points using trend indicators
2) Make two forecasts on entry and exit points, using oscillators;
3) Make two forecasts indicating divergences with all the items needed to confirm it.

CHAPTER 8. FIBONACCI LINES

I f you have already learned how to distinguish patterns on the price chart and also use various indicators and oscillators, determine divergences and convergences, then you cannot do without one more tool of technical analysis, namely the Fibonacci lines.

Fibonacci lines were invented by the first major Italian mathematician of medieval Europe, Leonardo of Pisa, better known as Fibonacci. This mathematician invented a certain sequence of numbers, which later were called Fibonacci numbers. The principle of these numbers is that each next number is found by adding up the two numbers before it: 1 + 1 = 2; 2 + 1 = 3; 3 + 2 = 5; 5 + 3 = 8; 8 + 5 = 13, etc.

Later, other numbers were derived from these numbers, which are used in trading.

What is so interesting about these numbers? They are based on the Golden Ratio principle which underpins almost everything that surrounds us. For example, the shell of many mollusks, sunflower seeds, flower petals, and even our auricle are formed according to the Golden Ratio principle.

The Fibonacci numbers based on the Golden Section principle have found use in trading because they describe not only the processes of development of the world but financial markets as well. This proves that the movement of prices is also subject to certain laws of the universe. The principle of Fibonacci numbers used in trading means each next number is divided into the previous one.

Many Fibonacci tools are used in trading:

- Fibonacci Retracement
- Fibonacci Expansion
- Fibonacci Fans
- Fibonacci Time Zones
- Periods of Fibonacci
- Fibonacci Circles
- Fibonacci Spiral
- Fibonacci Arcs
- Fibonacci Wedge
- Fibonacci Channel

We will pay attention to the first tool – Fibonacci Retracement. It is the most common tool for measuring the growth of a currency price or the extent of its correction (pullback).

So, we have already found out that the main task for which we use Fibonacci lines is the determination of price growth or pullback. Each increase in price is accompanied by a certain decrease, i.e., pullback, and at the same time, each pullback is followed by an increase. This is determined by means of Fibonacci lines.

Fibonacci lines themselves look like horizontal levels. They are underpinned by the basic Fibonacci coefficients (0.236, 0.382, 0.5, 0.618, 0.786, etc.). These lines can be drawn in Tradingview. Select theFibcoefficient tool in the taskbar (on the charts we'll consider the Fib Retracement tool) and extend the lines to the needed chart zone.

To measure pullback or growth, we select the minimum and maximum price points on the extreme wave of the current trend. With the correct application of this tool, the Fibonacci lines will help you determine strong support and resistance levels, which in turn will point to pullback goal or growth goal.

What do all these Fibonacci levels mean? These are the zones where traders place their buy or sell orders. Trading on Fibonacci lines is carried out from level to level. Fibonacci levels work due to human psychology. The greater number of traders pays attention to the same Fibonacci levels, the more pending orders are placed on these levels, making them stronger. That is, if traders see a Fibonacci level that coincides with the resistance line, they receive confirmation of their hypothesis and place orders.

Before we look at this tool on the chart, I want to draw your attention to some unwritten rules, which I recommend writing down:

1. On D1, the Fibonacci lines are built on closing prices
2. A genuine break through the level 0.382 signals fading of a trend and emerging of potential for reversal movement formation

3. The main application of Fibonacci lines is limited to an indication of minimum and maximum pullback zones
4. Targeted movement can continue without a pullback at least to a level of 0.236 only if there is some "doping" in form of news or force majeure events. In all other cases, the pullback will certainly occur
5. Bouncing off the level of 0.236 with a further achievement of new highs or lows occurs in 50 cases out of 100. In the remaining 50 cases, a pullback to the level of 0.382 will continue, where the probability of renewed targeted movement reaches a climax of 91%.

And now we will consider different types of pullbacks which can be measured on the chart.

50% Retracement

Note that on this chart the Fibonacci lines are extended from top to bottom, i.e., 0 is on the bottom, while 1 is on the top. Why is it so? There was a strong impulse for selling the currency at the maximum price point, so we need to measure further pullback, i.e., to understand how low the price may drop. When we get the first impulse for a drop in price, we see that the reversal movement (to growth) has reached the level of 0.5. On this level, sales continued to take place on the market. Later there was a retest, i.e., this level was once again tried to be overcome, but the price tumbled again.

38.2% Retracement

On this chart, the Fibonacci lines are extended differently than on the previous one. We have 1 on the bottom and 0 on the top. Here we stretch the Fibonacci lines to the impulse to determine the growth. Here the price approaches the level of 0.382, where buy orders are executed and the price goes upwards.

78.6% Retracement

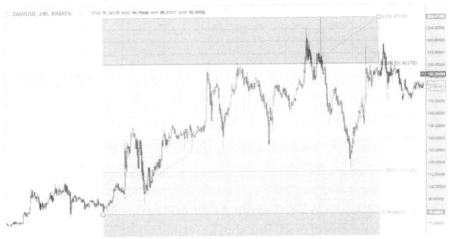

What do we see on this chart? To measure retracement, we take a lower, intermittent growth impulse. It is followed by retracement at the level of 0.786.

I can cite many such examples of retracement measurement, but let's now grasp the process of applying Fibonacci levels on the chart. We will look at two ways of extending Fibonacci lines.

The first thing you do when you open the chart (after determining the trend, is draw support and resistance levels) find the impulse on the top, i.e., the highest point of the most recent wave of the existing trend and the lowest point, i.e., the beginning of the trend on the bottom. You draw lines relying on these two points. Extend the Fibonacci lines from the lowest point to the highest point and thus measure to what Fibonacci level the price is retracing.

But be careful: this is the way the Fibonacci levels are extended by small potatoes, the crowd. But sharks – the large players – extend the Fibonacci lines differently. If the crowd extends the Fibonacci lines from the very bottom to the top, the sharks extend the lines from a point above the lowest one, where many "stops" occurred, i.e., the longest price movement on one horizontal level. We also should not reach the highest point on the top. That's how it looks.

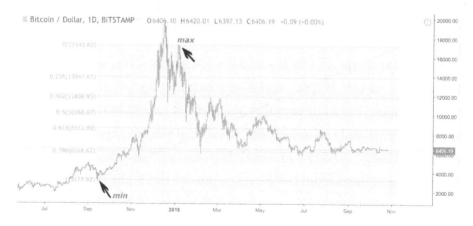

Why do the "sharks" extend the Fibonacci levels differently? They possess large capital and cannot leave the market with such assets at the very price peak. They leave at the point where a large amount of horizontal price movements is seen on the chart.

And one thing more: why do we need to extend the Fibonacci lines the same way as the "sharks" do? I will explain.

If you look at both charts, you will notice that the level of 0.618 on each of them is in different places. It is much lower on the crowd's chart. What does it mean? This means that the crowd will continue to bet on lower prices, i.e., open short positions. Thus it turns out that the large players just "make" small players to open short positions. As soon as the crowd opens many short positions, the "sharks" will move the market up.

Or there may be an opposite situation. The crowd buys a coin, thinking the price will bounce off the level 0.618 upwards. They open a long position and, of course, lose their money, as the price keeps falling. This is how the large players trick small players.

It's up to you to decide whether to believe in this theory about Fibonacci lines and major players or not. Let's continue puzzling out the topic.

Remember that the Fibonacci lines can help us measure not only the level to which the price will drop but also the level to which it will rise. Extend the Fibonacci lines from bottom to top (from the lower impulse to the higher one) during the growing market, and extend them from top to bottom during the falling market (to measure the pullback on purchase).

If you measure several impulse retracements on one area of the chart (and you can do so), the Fibonacci levels may crisscross sometimes. What does it mean? This means there is a very strong trading range in this area. You can also combine the Fibonacci lines you draw to determine growth with Fibonacci levels for determining a pullback. Their intersection will also show you the strong levels which you need to pay special attention to.

And now my main recommendation: set a take profit order not on the Fibonacci line itself, but at a distance of 5% before reaching the line. This will help you close the deal. Sometimes there are such situations when the price stops a few millimeters away from your level and reverses. Accordingly, your limit order will not be executed, but if your order waits for the price below the line, the probability of its execution increases significantly.

Another frequently asked question: Should Fibonacci lines be drawn on the highest points of candlesticks' bodies or upper shadows? We should capture upper shadows only if we work on a timeframe below 4 hours. However, we should bear in mind that there some shadows are manipulative in nature, for example, when there was no true movement in the market, but just some kind of panic buy or panic sell. Therefore, you should distinguish between the shadows or use a longer time frame.

One last recommendation on the subject of Fibonacci levels: *write down the perfect pairs of coins and levels. For example: "Litecoin works best on 0.382 level." Believe me, this will greatly help you in trading.*

Homework

1) Make 2-3 growth forecasts on Fibonacci levels, describe what each level means and what will be further developments of this coin

2) Make 2 Fibonacci forecasts on the highest point of candlestick's body (timeframe greater than 4h);

3) Make 2 Fibonacci forecasts on the highest point of candlestick's shadow (timeframe lower than 4h).

CHAPTER 9. JAPANESE CANDLESTICKS AND THEIR COMBINATIONS

How do most people visually imagine the price of an asset over time? I'm sure that most people imagine a wavy horizontal line that changes and curves up and down every second. In order to structure and give meaning to this constantly changing line, different types of price charts have been invented. The most popular types are Japanese candlesticks and bars.

Bars

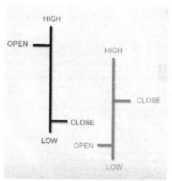

Western technical analysis

Japanese candlesticks

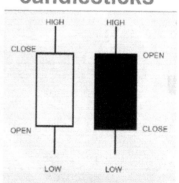

Eastern technical analysis

What is common between these two chart types?

Unlike the traditional linear chart, Japanese candlesticks and bars use as many as four data points for a given period of time instead of one:

1. The opening price when the time period began
2. The highest point the price reached during the time period
3. The lowest point the price reached in the period
4. The closing price when the period ended

It is these four points that increase the information value of the chart, which means they can immediately indicate what is happening in the market.

Bars are the tools of western technical analysis, whereas the Japanese candlesticks are the tools of eastern technical analysis. Bars can be of ascending or descending order, Japanese candlesticks can also be bullish or bearish. Both charts convey the same information.

If there is so much in common between these charts and they convey the same information, why do most traders prefer Japanese candlesticks? This tool has gained its popularity not only due to the simplicity of interpretation of the market situation but also because they reflect the gap between open price and a closing price of a candlestick. This area is called the real body of a candlestick. The body helps us to better assess the overall situation in the market presented on a chart.

Let's discuss the structure of Japanese candlesticks. A candlestick displays a range of price movement for a specific period of time (which we call a timeframe). A candlestick has a real body (it is usually painted black or white) and upper and lower shadows indicating the highest and lowest prices for a certain period.

Japanese candles come in three variations:

- Long body candlesticks
- Spinning Top and Paper Umbrella candlesticks
- Doji candlesticks

Long body candlesticks   Spinning top and Paper umbrella   Doji candlesticks
candlesticks

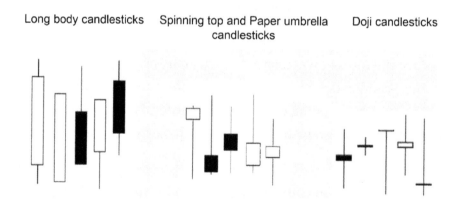

Long body candlesticks have very big bodies. A perfect long body candle also has minimal shadows. In this case, we understand that the price has a good direction. The smaller the shadow and the bigger the body are, the more reliable is the signal for us, which means that the market is heading in a certain direction.

You might ask: how can I identify a long body candlestick? Just compare the candlesticks with each other. You can identify a long body candlestick among other just by eye.

Spinning Top and Paper Umbrella candlesticks have a small body, while their shadow can be either large or small.

Doji candlesticks have a very small body or do not have it at all.

I am often asked which candlestick is better, i.e., more reliable? In principle, there are no "best candlesticks" in the market, because each of them provides a particular kind of information. For example, if we see long body candlesticks, we understand there is a purposeful and strong movement in the market. Long body candlesticks often break through the price range. That is, important levels are broken through with long body candlesticks. Patterns of technical analysis also usually break support or resistance level with long body candlesticks. Therefore, long body candlesticks are a kind of locomotive which drives the price. The rest of candlesticks (Spinning Top and Doji candlesticks) can form reversal candlestick configurations, indicating bouncing off a certain level and a trend reversal.

As for Doji candlesticks, they are considered to be uncertain in the market. Their body is small, and the open price is at the same point as the closing price. Nothing has changed in the market for this period of time. If we see a doji candlestick with an almost absent body and small shadow, it means that the price stands still and we are running in place. But if we see a doji candlestick with a small body and a big shadow, it can be a very strong signal. The nature of the signal depends on the direction of the shadow.

As for the trade volume, it can be seen only on large candlesticks in most cases.

Some Japanese candlesticks, which create certain combinations on the price chart, are called candlestick configurations (or candlestick patterns). They are divided into three types:

- Single candlestick patterns
- Dual candlestick patterns
- Triple candlestick patterns

Single candlestick and dual candlestick patterns enjoy the greatest popularity.

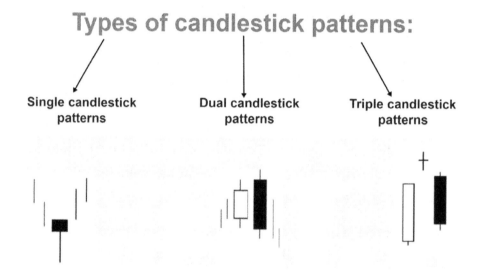

Types of candlestick patterns:

Single candlestick patterns

Dual candlestick patterns

Triple candlestick patterns

Single candlestick patterns

Single candlestick patterns, in turn, are divided into weak and strong. Strong configurations make it possible to interpret the direction of price movement with high probability and set pending orders. As soon as we see a strong candle configuration, we can open a position.

Weak configurations require additional confirmation. To make a final decision on opening a position, we will need one more candlestick of confirmation.

To date, there are a lot of books with a multitude of names of single candlestick patterns. However, we will deal with only the most frequently observed ones in the cryptocurrency market. At the same time, I do not recommend you to strain your brain to memorize the sophisticated names of all these candlestick configurations. You only need to grasp the principles of their formation.

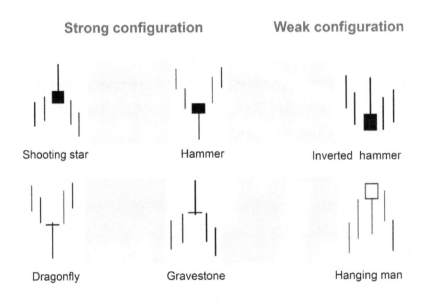

So, the shadows of all strong candlestick patterns are outside the previous price range. The shadows of all weak candlestick patterns are inside the pattern itself.

I do not recommend looking for candlesticks themselves somewhere in the middle of price ranges. We are interested in those candlesticks that are near important levels. The levels and lines determine the ranges where the price will move. As soon as the price reaches this level or line, we start to look for confirmation of breaking the level or bouncing off it. First we need the levels and lines, and then the candlesticks that confirm these or other signals. But do not forget that the candlesticks give us only a direction, while the levels, patterns or indicators show us our goal.

We view all classic candlestick configurations on the 30-minute time frame.

And now let's check ourselves a bit. There are two candlestick patterns below: Inverted Hammer and Shooting Star. Which one is strong and which one is weak?

Inverted Hammer is a weak pattern, and *Shooting Star* is a strong one. We could indicate this just by looking at the shadows of the patterns. In the first pattern, the shadow is inside; in the second pattern, it is outside.

Now let's define the weak and strong pattern on the following picture.

HANGING MAN

HAMMER

Hammer is a strong candlestick pattern, and *Hanging Man* is a weak one. (I hope that all my readers got that)

I suggest paying special attention to one single candlestick configuration as it differs from the others. It is called *Belt Hold Line* pattern and can be either bullish or bearish.

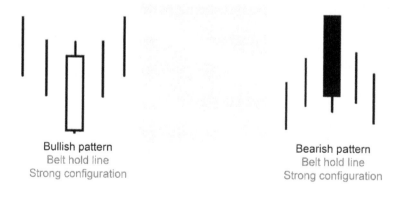

Bullish pattern
Belt hold line
Strong configuration

Bearish pattern
Belt hold line
Strong configuration

Bullish Belt Hold Line pattern is a strong configuration. This pattern has a long upward candlestick with the open price located at the level of the daily minimum. It has no lower shadow. *Bearish Belt Hold Line pattern* is also a strong configuration. It has a long downward candlestick with the open price at the level of the daily maximum. It has no upper shadow.

And finally, I want to warn you that single candlestick patterns can be called differently:

- Single candlestick configurations
- Pin bar
- Day breakout
- First-order extremum
- Spike

However, you should know these are only different names that do not change the function of these candlesticks in the market.

Dual candlestick patterns

Let's now puzzle out some *dual candlestick patterns.*

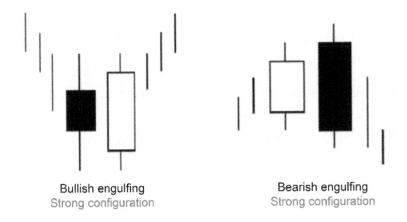

Bullish engulfing
Strong configuration

Bearish engulfing
Strong configuration

Bullish engulfing is a strong pattern. There should be a strong upward or downward trend in the market for its formation. This pattern is formed when a body of the second candlestick engulfs a body of the first candlestick, while the shadows may not be engulfed. The second body should be of contrasting color.

Bearish engulfing is also a strong candlestick pattern. It has the same characteristics as the previous one, only in a bear market.

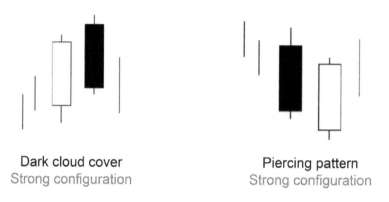

Dark cloud cover
Strong configuration

Piercing pattern
Strong configuration

Dark Cloud Cover is a strong pattern which consists of two candlesticks. The first one is a white candlestick with a strong body. The second one opens above the previous one. At the same time, it closes at the lowest point of the previous candle and covers a significant part of it.

Piercing Pattern is also a strong pattern and a mirror reflection of the Dark Cloud Cover pattern.

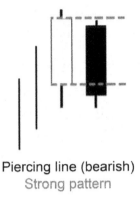

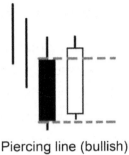

Piercing line (bearish)
Strong pattern

Piercing line (bullish)
Strong pattern

Piercing Line (bearish) is also a strong pattern. The second candlestick of this pattern opens lower than the first one closes. The second candlestick closes lower than the first one opens.

Piercing Line (bullish) is also a strong pattern. It is a mirror reflection of the previous pattern, just in a bull market.

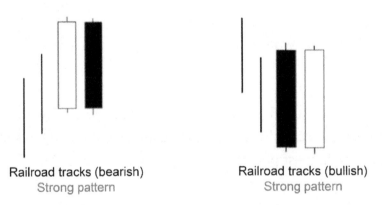

Railroad tracks (bearish)
Strong pattern

Railroad tracks (bullish)
Strong pattern

Railroad Tracks (bearish configuration) is a strong pattern. It consists of two almost identical candlesticks of contrasting colors. This candlestick pattern has large bodies and does not have long shadows.

Railroad Tracks (bullish configuration) is also a strong pattern. It has the same characteristics but appears in a bear market.

It is worth noting that there is one weak reversal pattern among all dual candlestick patterns. It is called Bearish Harami and Bullish Harami on the bottom of the market. The second candlestick of this configuration is very small, less than 50% of the previous one. It is also of contrasting color. The appearance of such a pattern on the chart should at least make you look at the current market situation.

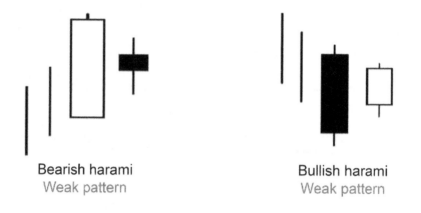

Bearish harami
Weak pattern

Bullish harami
Weak pattern

There is also a so-called "booster" of configurations: *Tweezer.* It consists of two candlesticks of contrasting colors with the same lowest and highest points.

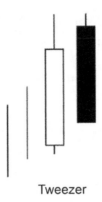

Tweezer

Tweezer is not a separate configuration. It gives additional strength to the signal we received. Tweezer alone cannot be a strong signal of a trend reversal; its role is to reinforce one or another candlestick pattern. Therefore, Tweezer can be found on the chart in a pair with different patterns.

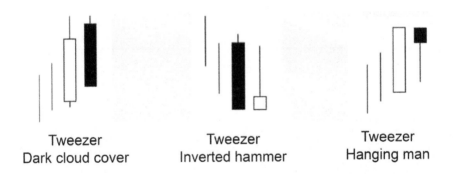

Tweezer
Dark cloud cover

Tweezer
Inverted hammer

Tweezer
Hanging man

We touched upon the main candlestick configurations observed in the cryptocurrency market. Do not try to memorize all their names. The main thing you need to learn: the main factor in single candlestick patterns is the shadow; the main factor in dual candlestick configurations is the size and the color of candlestick's body. Shadows in dual candlestick configurations are not important, but still, the shorter they are, the better.

If you analyze the Japanese candlesticks on the chart, stick to the following rules:

1. Estimate the size, color, and configuration of a candlestick only after it is closed
2. Size of a candlestick is a subjective indicator as it depends on the current market volatility
3. Examine the reversal candlestick patterns turning on the top or on the bottom of the market
4. Do not forget that reversal candlestick patterns indicate only the price reversal, not how far the price will reach
5. The larger the timeframe is, the more reliable the signal of candlestick patterns.

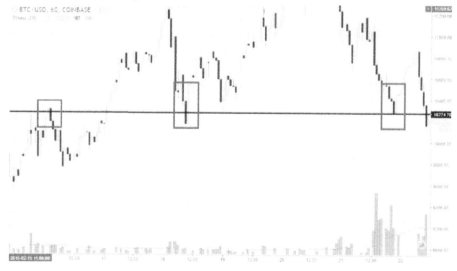

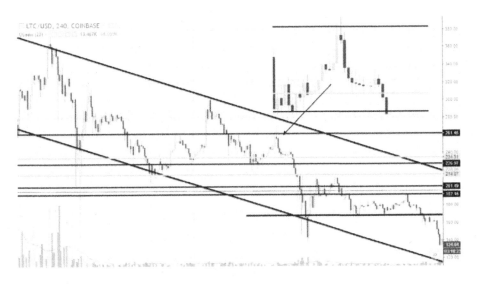

At the same time, Japanese candlesticks are also estimated by the body strength, the shadow strength, and negative strength.

Body strength: The longer the body is, the higher the likelihood of price movement in the selected direction.

Shadow strength: the shorter the shadow is, the higher the likelihood of movement towards the short shadow.

Negative strength: if the price has not moved in the expected direction, it is most likely to go in the opposite direction.

Homework

1) Make two forecasts, using single candlestick configurations

2) Make two forecasts, using dual candlestick configurations

CHAPTER 10. ELLIOTT WAVE THEORY OR WAVE TRADING

Some traders believe the Elliott Wave Theory to be the best tool for determining market movement. I will tell you: hold off on rejoicing as if you found a panacea for all woes. First, you have to spend more than one day of your life to comprehend the wave theory since this tool is complex. Second, I still prefer to take into account data from several tools during the analysis of the chart of the selected coin. The rest is up to you.

What is the Elliott Wave Theory? In brief, Elliott waves make it possible to structure complex and chaotic movements in the market. How?

I am sure you know there are growth phases and decline phases in the market. And it is the Elliott Wave Theory that can structure all these phases on a chart.

Before we plunge into the difficult topic of the Elliott waves, I suggest recalling once again the basics of technical analysis. You may use the Elliott Wave Theory, the indicators, graphical analysis or not, these rules work the same for all the instruments.

The Dow theory says:

- Market takes into account everything

- Market moves in a certain direction
- Volume confirms trend
- Trends exist until definitive signals prove that they have ended

Jesse Livermore's rules:

- Nothing new never occurs in the business of speculating or investing
- Markets are never wrong – opinions often are
- Avoid get-rich-quick schemes
- Wishful thinking must be banished

These classics outlined some of the fundamental principles of technical analysis, where the Elliot Wave Theory holds its prominent place. Therefore, I recommend each of these rules be remembered at all costs.

The next thing you need to learn to grasp the Elliott Wave Theory is the cyclic, phase and fractal nature of financial markets. Get ready: there will be a lot of charts now, but we can't do without them in this section.

On the Bitcoin chart for 2017, we can see both the growth phase and the price decline phase in the first half of the year. However, at the end of August and the beginning of September, the price chart formed a new growth phase of and new decline phase. At the same time, at the end of the year, another phase of rapid growth and decline phase appeared. What does it mean? This means that Bitcoin moved very well in certain cycles last year.

On this chart, you can better see how the price influenced on forming of the growth phase proceeded with the decline phase, i.e., it formed a whole market cycle.

This picture shows a gold price chart. It demonstrates an example of *phasal and cyclic nature of the price*. Note that the cyclic nature is observed within the growth phase (as well as the decline phase), i.e., smaller growth phases and smaller decline phases. Thus, we understand that every big wave has a smaller sub-waves.

And here I tried to demonstrate the *fractal nature* of the market. We can observe the main wave as well as its internal structure in the growth phase. The decline phase is also divided into sub-waves.

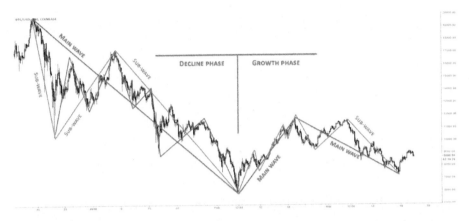

If we talk about this chart, it shows a decline phase as the Bitcoin price formed a downward wave in early 2018. Here the main waves are also divided into sub-waves.

Thus, we have figured out how the phasal and fractal nature looks like on the price chart. Now let's take a closer look at the Elliott Wave Theory itself.

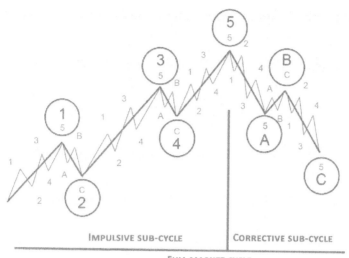

A growth phase in the Elliott Wave Theory is called *impulsive sub-cycle*, while the decline phase is called *corrective sub-cycle*. The two phases form a *full market cycle*.

Impulsive sub-cycle usually consists of 5 waves, where waves 1, 3 and 5 are impulses and waves 2 and 4 are correctional waves that link these impulses. Each wave also has an internal wave structure where, for example, impulse wave 1 is built from 5 waves, correctional wave 2 is built from 3 waves, impulse wave 3 is built from 5 waves, wave 4 is built from 3 waves and the last 5 wave has a five-wave structure.

Now let's consider a corrective sub-cycle, which has a three-wave structure. It is marked as wave A, wave B, and wave C. the impulse waves are waves A and C, and the correctional connecting wave is wave B. Waves A and C also have the internal wave structure: each of them has 5 sub-waves. The correctional wave B has a three-wave structure.

Take a look at this chart. Pay attention that the impulse wave 5 was extended on the Bitcoin chart for 2017. The peak of trading activity was observed in this range. Wave 5 demonstrated well that Bitcoin was overbought at that time. Therefore, when analyzing a coin chart, always pay attention to wave 5. If it has risen too much upwards (it looks too "sharp"), it means that the price chart is overbought. If you see a pronounced five-wave structure, it is a good signal for you to refrain from buying and make a certain pause. After all, the price chart is likely to reverse after this period, so you should focus on the decline.

If you have carefully examined the chart above (especially its decline phase), you should have a question: "What is the offshoot after wave C, which is the last in the decline phase?" It is the beginning of a new phase of the upward movement.

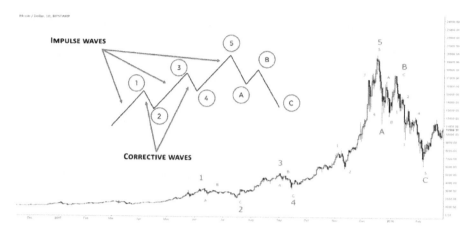

On this picture, you can once again see how impulse and corrective waves are combined on the price chart.

And now let's consider the basic rules of Elliott Wave Theory:

1. Wave 2 never reaches the beginning of wave 1
2. Wave 3 is never the shortest one
3. Wave 4 never intrudes into the area of wave 1

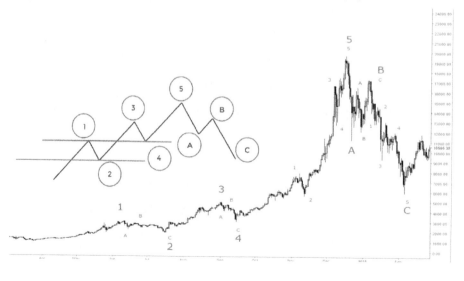

I need to mention that there are, of course, exceptions in the market. After all, these rules were developed by Ralph Nelson Elliott at the beginning of the last century.

Impulse waves

Now let's consider *impulse waves* and their practical application.

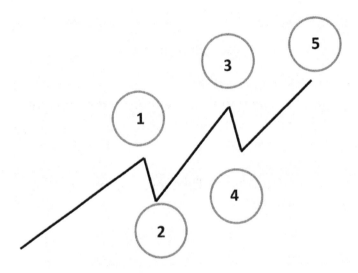

Impulse waves are not always identical, but there are still general rules to indicate them:

1. Each subsequent peak of impulse wave is higher than the previous one
2. Impulse wave has five sub-waves.

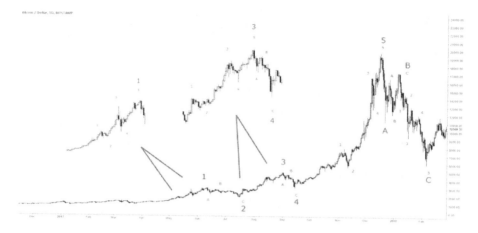

Here's an example. The impulses are indicated on this Bitcoin price chart. Impulse wave 1 and impulse wave 3 have a five-wave structure.

Still, what are the exceptions? The most common is the *impulse extension*.

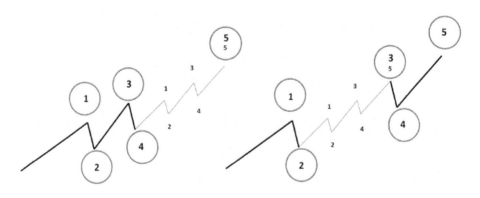

The impulse extension is characterized by:

1. Impulse wave is abnormally long
2. Often observed in wave 3 and wave 5
3. The last sub-wave may be the shortest one

We can observe an example of such an extension on the Bitcoin chart for 2017, where the impulse wave 5 was abnormally long.

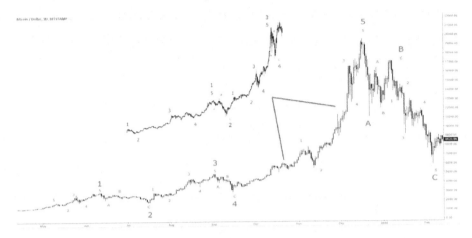

And now we will consider another unconventional, but interesting case, which can be seen in the market on rare occasions: *impulse wave truncation.*

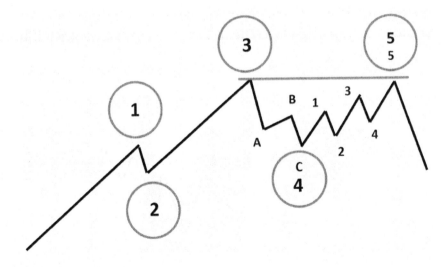

It is characterized by:

1. Last wave 5 does not go beyond the peak of impulse wave 3
2. Five-wave structure is inside truncated wave 5

If you see such a structure on the chart, i.e., the impulse wave truncation will occur, you should know this is a reliable signal of a trend reversal.

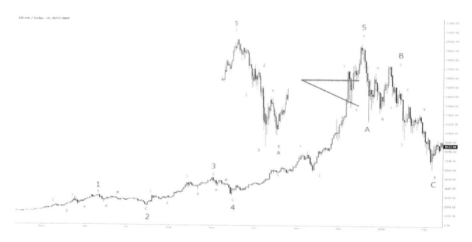

The next structure is the *diagonal triangle*. It resembles the truncation of the fifth wave. The difference is that it occurs within a diagonal triangle.

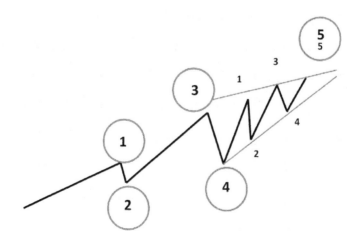

It is characterized by:

1. The last fifth wave is higher than the third impulse wave
2. Five-wave structure is inside the diagonal triangle

The appearance of a diagonal triangle on the chart signals completion of an upward trend.

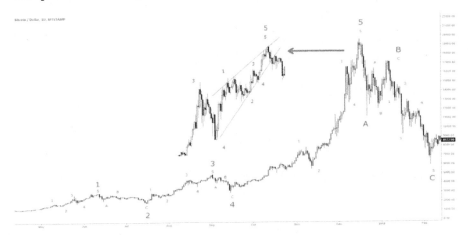

Here is an example of the diagonal triangle on the top of the last wave 5. It is an obvious Bitcoin overbought zone. The third wave turned out to be the shortest here, but nevertheless, its peak is above the peak of impulse wave 1.

Corrective waves

As we have considered all the variations of impulse waves, let's now move on to *corrective waves.*

These waves are, perhaps, the most complicated in the Elliott Wave Theory since there is a large number of such waves and it's easy to get them mixed up. Therefore, based on my personal experience, I advise determining the Elliott correctional waves in combination with graphical analysis and other trading tools.

The first corrective wave under consideration is a Zigzag correction. It is characterized by:

1. Wave C is below wave A
2. The formula of sub-waves is 5-3-5, i.e., wave A has a five-wave structure; wave B has a three-wave structure; wave C has a five-wave structure.

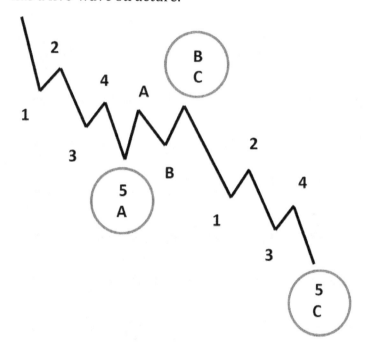

Let's consider an example of zigzag correction on a chart.

This is an example of zigzag correction, where wave C is below wave A.

Flat correction. This wave is determined as follows:

1. Wave C is at the level of wave A
2. The formula of sub-waves is 3-3-5

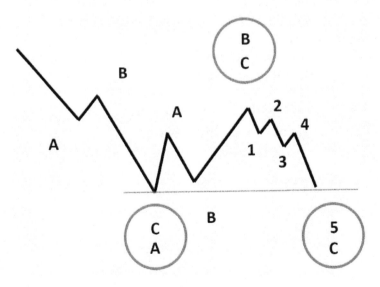

In my opinion, a flat correction is one of the most difficult corrections to identify correctly, since false corrections are common (when wave B may go beyond the peak of the previous impulse, but wave C will not go below impulse wave A).

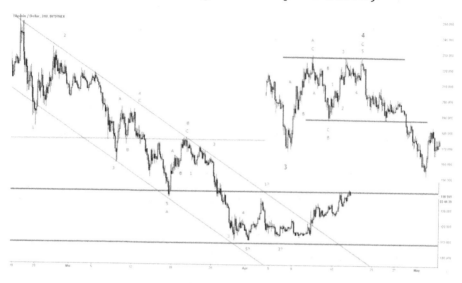

Here is a good example of flat correction. It is a side correction within the downward trend.

The next wave is *running correction*:

1. Wave C is above the level of wave A
2. The formula of sub-waves is 3-3-5.

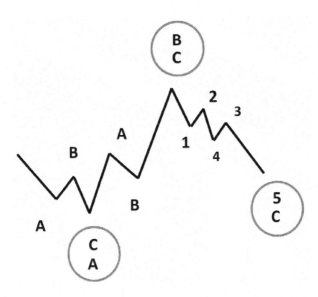

Running correction is often observed during an uptrend. If you see that wave C is the shortest one and does not reach wave A during an uptrend, it's already a good signal that the price chart can bounce off the support level and go further upwards forming a new impulse.

Triangle is a complicated structure within the framework of the Elliott Wave Theory. It is characterized by:

- Observed in corrections
- Has five-wave structure in the Elliott Wave Theory
- Wave E signals to exit from pattern
- Structure of sub-waves is 3-3-3-3-3

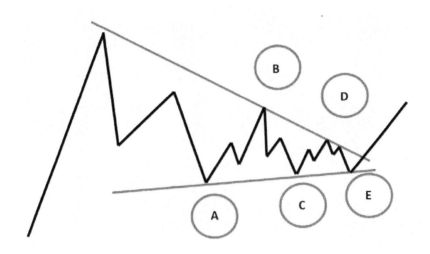

Here is an example of a good wave triangle.

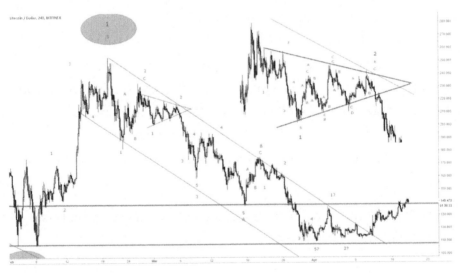

Combined corrections can also be found on the cryptocurrency price chart.

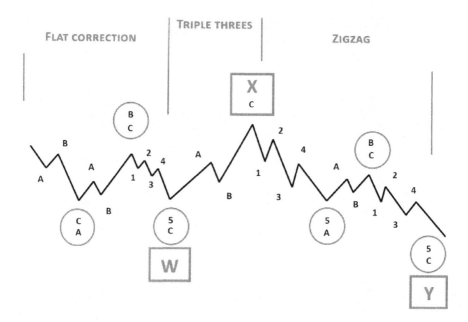

Personally, I have observed combined structure built from flat correction, where wave C does not go beyond the bottom of wave A, followed by connecting correction within the triple threes, and then a zigzag, which as a rule serves as a closing formation in combined structures. Such wave formation has the shape of WXY. This corrective movement happens rarely, but it takes a long time to form.

Here is an example of a combined correction structure on Dash coin / USD price chart.

Compatibility of Elliott waves with other forecasting tools

We have already considered the varieties of waves. Let's now discuss the *compatibility of the Elliott Wave Theory with the levels of Fibonacci number sequence*. It's a very extensive topic, but we will focus on the most important points.

By the way, many of my fellow traders use Elliott waves combined with Fibonacci lines. Therefore, make yourself comfortable and read carefully.

The Fibonacci grid is extended on the price chart in the direction of a downtrend from 100% to 0%. If the price reaches the area of the golden section during the corrective movement (the levels of 61.8% and 50%), which at the same time are strong, it is a confident reversal signal.

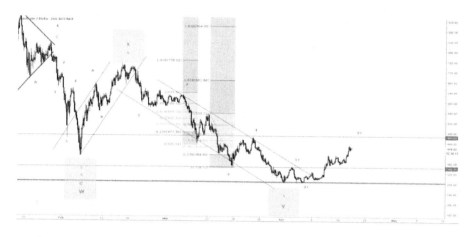

The Fibonacci extension can be applied during both uptrend and downtrend.

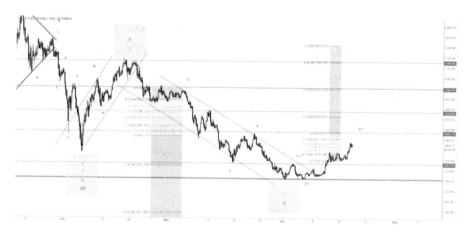

Now let's consider an example of how to *combine the Elliott Wave Theory with complex technical analysis.*

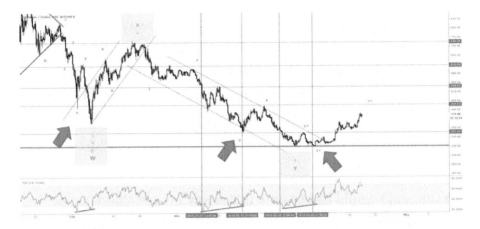

On the chart, I combined the Elliott Wave Theory with the RSI oscillator, which, as you know, shows not only local overbought or oversold zones, but the divergence and convergence as well. Therefore, if the Elliott waves seem complicated to you and you are not sure in your forecasts, it won't be difficult to find divergence with the help of this oscillator. Divergence will confirm the correctness (or incorrectness) of your forecast.

We can also add a moving average to the Elliott waves and the RSI oscillator. The more signals we receive, the better.

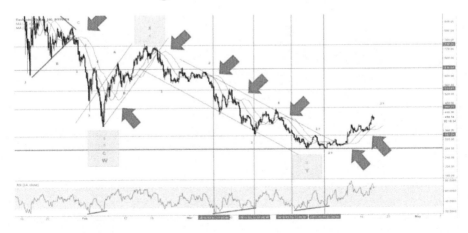

As for a suitable time frame for drawing Elliott waves, I, as always, recommend using a "large to small" principle: first, for example, we analyze the monthly chart, then the weekly chart, and then the daily chart. Thus you can see a growth phase and a decline phase in detail. Look for main waves on large timeframes; look for internal wave structure (confirmation of the main waves) on smaller time frames.

To sum up, I would like to note that many people characterize Elliott Wave Theory as an exotic part of technical analysis. Nevertheless, an increasing number of traders resort to this "exotic" tool. Indeed, Elliott waves are complicated but very efficient. They teach you how to structure the price chart, and the more practice you have with waves, the clearer they will be for you.

Homework

1) Find a growth phase and a decline phase on a D1 timeframe of three cryptocurrency charts. Mark the impulse movement with numbers 1, 2, 3, 4 and 5; mark the corrective movement with letters A, B, and C

2) Find extension and truncation of impulse wave on H4 or H1 timeframe of three cryptocurrency charts.

3) Find zigzag, sideway or running correction (in impulse or corrective wave) on H4 or H1 timeframe of three cryptocurrency charts

4) Make a small explanation of your observations (no more than two paragraphs) below each chart

CHAPTER 11. TRADING ON BREAKOUTS OF LOCAL TOPS AND IMPORTANT LEVELS

Many traders consider breakout trading to be a separate trading strategy. No matter what you call it, it will work when you master its specifics. Although this topic is simple (compared to the Elliott Wave Theory), it still has many peculiarities worth grasping at the early stage. So, let's get started.

You already understand that financial markets move in a focused manner. If we observe that the price chart moves towards the upward trend, where each next low is higher than the previous one, and market participants buy more than sell, we get good trading signals in this case. That is, we are confident that the market participants will continue to buy.

If we observe a downward trend, where each new low is lower than the previous one, then we understand that traders will continue to focus on lowering price.

To determine the willingness of the price to move in a certain direction, many traders use the highs and lows of the chart.

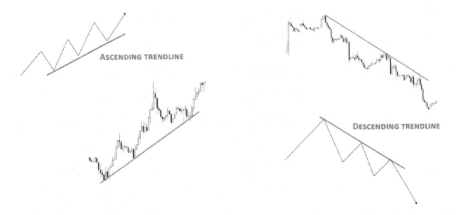

Let's look at an example of how you can get an additional entry point just on breakouts of local tops.

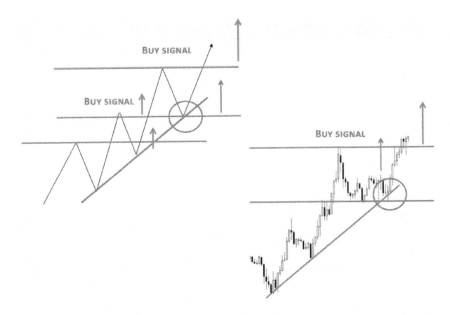

If the price chart not only bounces off the ascending trend line, where we have identified local tops but also crosses them, we receive an additional signal. In the picture on the left, the bottommost arrows indicate that we receive a buy signal even after bouncing off the support level. But if you need a more reliable signal, you should wait for a new local top.

Those traders who trade quickly after the first signal are the aggressive traders, who tend to take risks. You may ask: Why is it risky if the price bounced off the support level? Remember that false breakouts can occur in the market. Besides, the news background can break your uptrend in one minute. That is why such traders take risks. However, those who wait for the second signal are proponents of a more moderate trading style. They prefer waiting until the price chart reaches a new high and then making their purchase.

Below I will give another example of when the price chart not only bounces off the ascending trend line but also continues to go up, forming a local top.

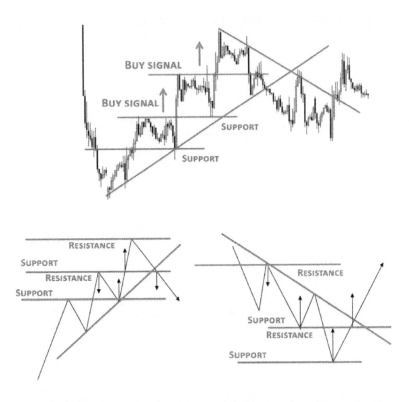

And now let's take a closer look at the ascending and descending tops.

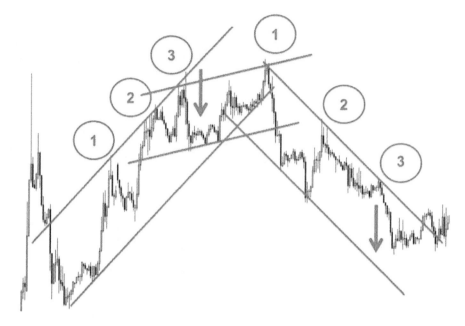

Consider how you can use a pending buy order during the breakout of the local top.

We get a buy signal even when we notice that, although the price chart has slightly retraced after the next peak, it still did not go below the moving average. We place a pending order above the resistance level. As soon as the local top is breached, the price chart will reach your pending order.

As a rule, the breakout of a local top is followed by an acceleration of the upward trend, so I recommend using a pending order in order to take your profit.

If you still have some doubts about your forecast, you can put a stop loss below the support level and thus protect yourself from unnecessary losses.

And here is an example of how you can use pending orders when you trade using the Elliott Wave Theory.

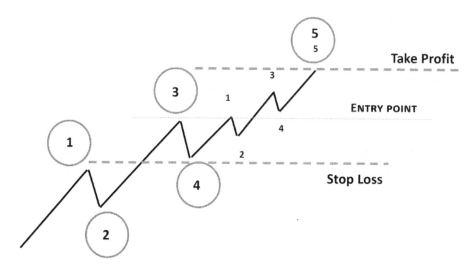

If the price chart has already formed impulse wave 1 and corrective wave 2, then impulse wave 3 and corrective wave 4, it is easy to guess that the market can go further upwards since the price chart is in the upward movement phase. We place a pending buy order slightly above the impulse wave 3 and expect the completion of a five-wave movement within the framework of wave 5. Place Take Profit depending on your patience (or greed :-). As for Stop Loss, put it a little below the corrective wave 4.

Here is an example of how you can make money during the corrective phase of the price chart.

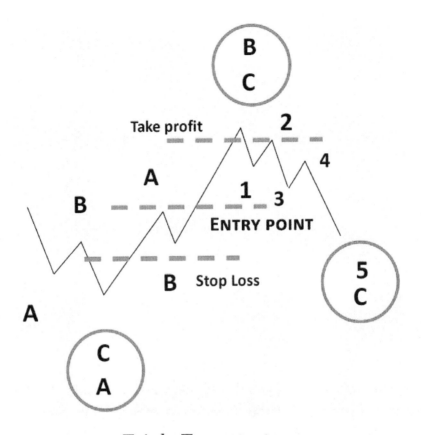

Triple Taps strategy

Now we proceed to an interesting strategy called "Triple Taps." It reveals the topic of trading on the breakout of local tops.

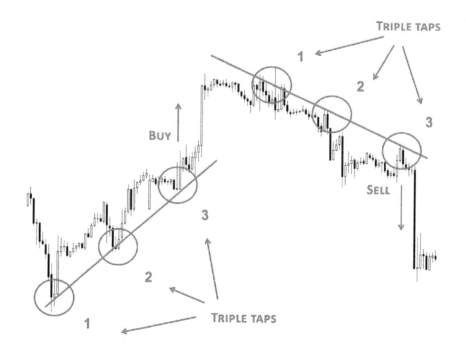

The most important thing in this strategy is to determine the level correctly. If you see that your level is tested repeatedly (three price taps are obvious), the uptrend is often accelerated then after the third tap.

The same things, but in the inverse manner, happen during a downtrend: the price chart lowers and three taps of the level are formed, followed by downtrend acceleration.

This chart shows that we receive an accurate signal for making a transaction after the last third price tap. In this situation, it is also possible to enter both after breaking a line and after forming a local top or even after breaking this top.

To get a more reliable forecast, the Triple Taps strategy can be combined with the Fibonacci tools.

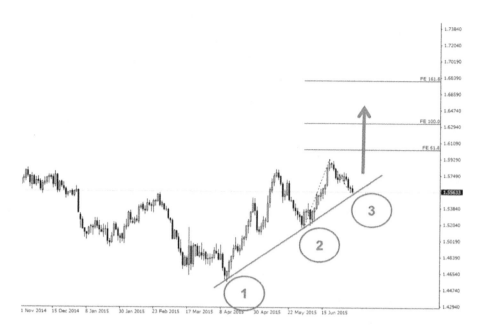

After the third tap, we extend the Fibonacci lines from the second tap to a local top further to the third tap. Thus, we will see where the price chart can reach in case of its further growth.

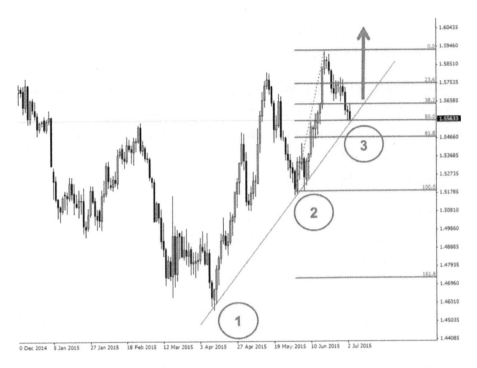

And the last example. Here the third tap took place in the golden section area according to the Fibonacci Retracement tool. The price reached the area of 38.2%, fixed in the area of 50% and even has a pullback to the area of 61.8%. This signal shows that the corrective movement may end.

Now let's summarize. The principle of trading on breakouts of local tops and important levels is simple and clear. If you want to trade in the market, expect the breakout of a local top. If you are willing to wait a bit because you do not want to trade aggressively, use a pending order on the breakout of this local top. If you want to trade from the top to the top, choose the Triple Taps trading strategy. If you fear the price will not break the level of the third tap, place a pending order to buy after the breakout of this level.

When the chart breaks the level, you will be calm as you are already in a higher price range.

Remember that this trading strategy seems to be very simple and easy at first glance. In fact, its main hitch is hidden in a large number of false breakouts when the price breaks the level but then comes back. This makes a large number of traders, especially beginners, lose their capital.

My advice in this case (though I recommend doing this almost in every section of my book) is not to use only one tool to forecast price movements. You should combine several tools.

Homework

1) Find reference points for placing take profit and stop loss orders after the third tap of defining level on H1 or H4 timeframe (this practical task will teach you to determine the nearest highs and lows so that you will be able to place stop loss and take profit orders)

2) Use Fibonacci extension within the Triple Taps from the low of wave 2 (second tap) to the low of wave 4 (third tap) on H1 or H4 timeframe. The purpose of this assignment is to learn how to find the potential of movement during the break of the important level

3) Make a small explanation of your observations below each chart.

CHAPTER 12. COMBINED APPLICATION OF TECHNICAL ANALYSIS TECHNIQUES

I was not sure whether I should include this section in my book. At first glance, this topic may seem to be unworthy of separate discussion. However, in my opinion, it is important. Moreover, the combined application of technical analysis techniques is one of my main approaches to making a trading decision. I consider this approach to be flawless as it gives a lot of additional signals, and the more we have, the better. So, add my tips to your armory.

You have already guessed that this section obliges us to repeat almost all the information we have already learned. Let's start from the basics of the technical analysis. I have mentioned that the basic rule of technical analysis is "History repeats itself." Nothing new happens in the financial markets. Everything that has ever happened is bound to happen in the future again. Therefore, whatever tool of technical analysis you use, remember this rule.

It can't hurt to once again recall some basics of trend formation. If we see the price chart follows an uptrend, the next high should be higher than the previous one. Thus, a kind of ladder is built in front of us, which shows where the price chart can go further. If we talk about the Elliott Wave Theory, this ladder should be called the "growth phase."

During a downtrend, the opposite is true: each next high should be lower than the previous one.

If we draw support and resistance levels below and above the price chart, we get the channel. Thus, the channel consists of two parallel lines, between which a price chart lies.

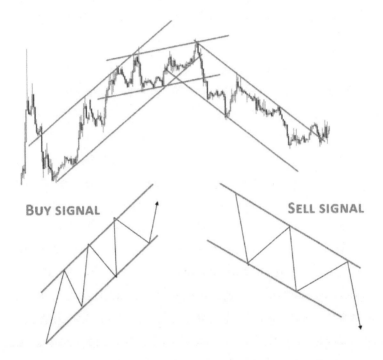

Support is the level at which prices are controlled by buyers, who prevent their further drop.

Resistance is the level at which prices are controlled by sellers, who prevent further rise.

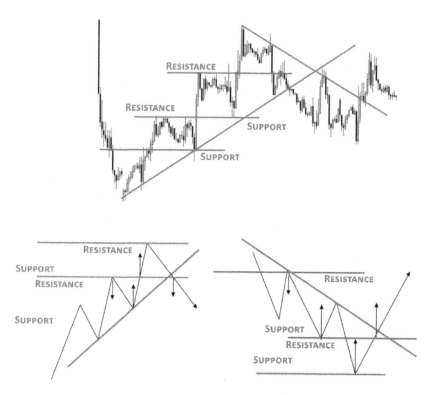

If the price bounces off an uptrend and the price chart crosses an important resistance level, i.e., a local top, then we receive two signals: the first – bouncing off the support level during an uptrend, and the second - a signal on the breakout of a local top. The first signal is suitable for those traders, who are willing to trade aggressively, while the second one is for those, who prefer trading in a more moderate and conservative manner.

And now let's consider, the simplest complex of technical analysis techniques - the use of support and resistance levels with moving averages.

The chart shows that the price has formed an upward channel. The support and resistance levels are indicated inside the channel. Thus, we have a buy signal for making transaction inside the channel with a target to the next level. Moreover, an additional argument is finding a moving average below the price chart, which gives technical confirmation in favor of a successful deal. In other words, if the price crosses the moving averages, and they, in turn, also cross each other to signal growth, then it is a very reliable signal showing we should expect a new wave of growth. In this case, our buy signals are a bounce off the moving averages and a bounce off a trend.

Let's consider some more interesting examples of how you can put into practice the elements of graphical analysis together with moving averages.

We see that the price chart crossed the trend support line and exited an upward trend. Besides this, the price chart went below the moving averages, which, in turn, crossed to signal a sale. In the chart below we see another crossover of moving averages and trend line reversal. It is another signal of downtrend continuation.

Here is another example of the signals we receive thanks to the combined application of levels with moving averages.

Now it's time to touch upon the combined application of Fibonacci tools and moving averages. Do not forget that Fibonacci numbers play an important role in forecasting price movements.

When the price chart is retraced against the previous upward movement, it is important to determine the "golden section" zone. There are ongoing disputes among traders: where is the "golden section" zone located? Some think it is located at the level of 38.2%, someone else believes it is the level of 50%, others claims it is 61.8%. Personally, I think that the "golden section" area is the range between 38.2% and 61.8%. And the farther the price chart enters this range, the higher is the probability of price reversal. This is how we can find a reversal point.

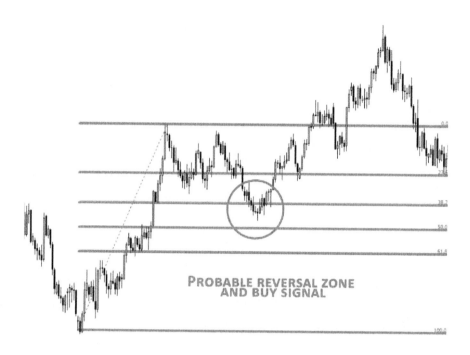

PROBABLE REVERSAL ZONE
AND BUY SIGNAL

Here is an example of a combined application of Fibonacci tools and moving averages.

MA CROSSOVER

CONSOLIDATION AND REVERSAL
FROM 0.382 LEVEL AND MA SIGNAL

And now let's grasp how you can use the Relative Strength Index (RSI) along with the trend lines. Let me remind you that the RSI indicator tops are usually formed above 70%, while the bottoms are formed below 30% and they lead the formation of tops and bottoms on the price chart.

As soon as the indicator chart goes beyond the signal line, for example, in the zone of 30%, we understand that a coin is oversold at the moment. If the indicator's chart reaches the zone of 70%, it means that a coin is overbought and, therefore, the opposite movement can be expected.

The picture shows that the price chart was trying to reach local resistance but failed to cross this level and dropped. Note that when the price chart tested the resistance level, the indicator chart was in the overbought area. Then we see that the indicator chart went to the oversold area.

Here are examples of divergence and convergence on RSI indicator, which are used together with trend lines.t

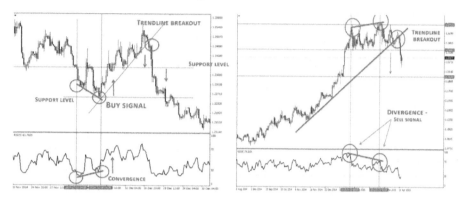

To forecast the price movement, it is also good to combine the reversal patterns with the RSI indicator. Practice shows that the top of the head of a pattern sometimes may be very overbought, which is signaled by RSI index. However, the patterns may give signals of divergence.

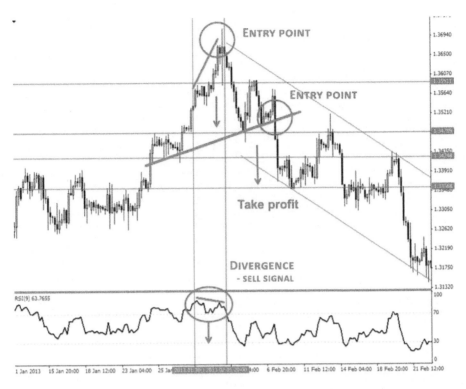

So, we see the Head and Shoulders reversal pattern at the top of the chart. It is obvious that the RSI index does not agree with the further growth of the currency pair. During the formation of price chart tops, where the next peak was higher than the previous one, the RSI index showed the opposite situation, which is also called a mirror. Divergence formed. Thus, we received a signal that the asset would leave the trading range and head to confident sales. Note that an additional sell signal also showed a break of a pattern's neckline.

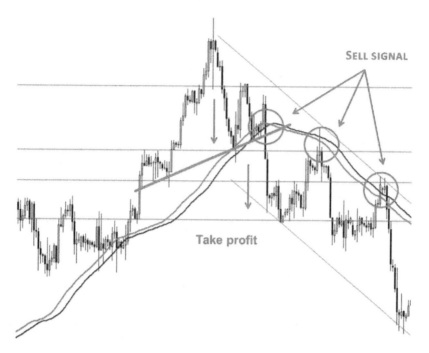

SELL SIGNAL

Take profit

Through this example, we observe a double trend reversal signal and a confirmed sell signal. After the Head and Shoulders pattern was formed, the moving averages crossover above the signal line was an additional sell signal from the neckline. Thus, a signal to downtrend formation with further sale priority appeared. After the trading asset formed a downtrend, moving averages served as a kind of resistance against reversal.

And finally, let's consider how you can use trend continuation patterns along with moving averages.

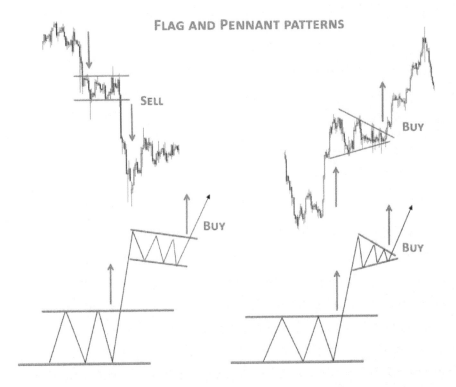

Flag and Pennant patterns signify short pauses in a developing trend. The formation of these patterns on the chart is preceded by a steep and almost straight line of price movement. They designate a market that in its development up or down gets ahead of itself so it pause for a moment before continuing to move in the same direction. If the price chart has formed an impulse followed by consolidation, it doesn't matter whether the price will be within a Flag or a Pennant pattern as we still expect a movement equal to the height of the previous impulse movement.

Flag and Pennant patterns are among the most reliable trend continuation patterns. Breakout of the trend in these patterns is extremely rare.

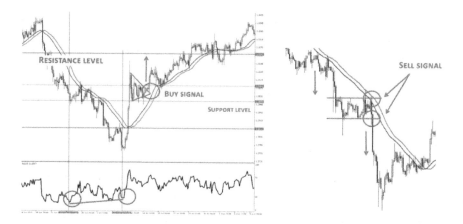

As for combining the trend continuation patterns with moving averages: if you, for example, see a Pennant trend continuation pattern on the chart, while the price does not go below the moving average but tries to fix in the higher ranges, it's a good buy signal. But if you see that the price chart is ready to get out of the consolidated movement within a Flag pattern, while the price bounces off the moving average, it's a good confirmation that the price chart can hit a target during the downward movement.

These are simple examples of a combined application of technical analysis techniques we have mastered. A more detailed scheme of combining various tools for coin analysis is called "trading strategy." We are going to deal with this topic in the next section.

Homework

1) Find all reversal patterns you know on H1 or H4 timeframe. Mark at least two trading signals for each cryptocurrency along with the RSI index

2) Find all trend continuation patterns you know on H1 or H4 timeframe. Mark at least two trading signals for each cryptocurrency along with moving average indicators.

Note: Remember that patterns on the chart may differ significantly from the perfect patterns shown in trading manuals.

CHAPTER 13. DEVELOPING TRADING SYSTEMS

M ake yourself comfortable and read carefully: now (thankfully or not) there will be fewer charts and more text.

Since cryptocurrency is a unique financial instrument, it requires a specific approach to choosing a trading strategy. Yes, I do not discount that many traders at the beginning of their "career" trade intuitively, but in the end, having lost the certain sum of money, they come to the conclusion they need to develop a certain list of trading rules and to adhere to them. These rules constitute a trading system.

Everyone can succeed in cryptocurrency trading at least once, but very few people can maintain a stable profitable system. What do these few people do to yield such a result? They develop the correct trading strategy. I want to underscore: CORRECT, not PERFECT.

Many of my students for some reason believe that I, like other successful traders, have some kind of secret strategy serving like a money-machine. They imagine me sitting with a glass of wine, pressing some buttons, while bitcoins pour into my wallet. Do you believe in this too? If so, I am going to disappoint you.

If you believe in a "perfect" trading strategy, then you have a good chance of taking the bait of by no means perfect guys who have recently been multiplying at an exponential rate. They are promoting at every step their super-duper secret strategy claiming it will "easily" augment your cryptocurrency in exchange for a very "insignificant and modest" sum. Beware of such trading "gurus"! Put your thinking cap on: why would a successful trader share secret information with you? Do you think he or she will sell you a golden goose for 2 pennies?

You may argue that many traders consistently make good money. Yes, but they make their money thanks to CORRECT, not PERFECT strategy.

Why am I telling you all this? I want you to learn once and for all: there are no magic pills, including for trading. It is impossible to find a marvelous strategy that will help you to magnify capital gains on the fly. Therefore, if you hoped this book would give you a clear step-by-step algorithm for becoming a cryptocurrency millionaire in the shortest time possible, you can close this book right now. Do not continue wasting your time. This book is for thoughtful traders who are willing to take knowledge and transform it into their own trading decisions. These decisions should not be mine, but yours and only yours!

I advise you to once again reread the last few sentences and memorize them forever. Strange as it may sound, they are the secret of successful trading.

Now, let's figure out what a "trading system" is.

A trading system (decision-making system) is a set of rules which a trader uses in the market. These rules can be either written down on paper or kept in mind. The most important thing is that the system a trader uses should be the most suitable one for his or her requirements. This depends on many parameters:

Temper. You choose what is more acceptable for you: short-term trading (several transactions per day), medium-term trading (from several transactions per day to one or two transactions per week) or long-term trading (several transactions per year)

Risk tolerance: what do you prefer: a lot of frequent and minor losses or rare and large losses?

Time. Determine how much time you can devote to trading. For example, short-term trading can take all your working time, while medium-term and long-term trading requires looking at a chart once a day

Trading capital. Evaluate what size of capital you have. You should have enough funds on your trading account for implementing your system. Different systems require a different size of start-up capital

Your knowledge about the market. Most decision-making systems are built using approaches and techniques of technical analysis. Therefore, you just need a basic knowledge of price chart analysis.

The most important thing is that all these points should not characterize you as a member of a certain category of traders, but first of all teach you to adhere to your own rules. If you follow them consistently and do not deviate from the chosen path, you will come to make a profit.

Before we start to sort out specific trading systems, I want to focus on one more thing. Having chosen a certain trading system, a trader sooner or later faces the fact that their "flawless" strategy starts to inflict losses. What conclusions does the trader make? It is necessary to optimize the system! A trader eliminates a problem (for example, by retuning the indicators slightly) and hopes that now everything will go smoothly and there will be no more unprofitable transactions. But what a rotten luck! The already "corrected" system continues to cause damage. A trader again optimizes the existing system and continues to trade, losing money. This process is ongoing until a trader loses patience (or capital).

What should such a trader do? Stop and analyze the causes of damages. Perhaps, this will help come to the conclusion that optimizing the system was not the best solution.

The cryptocurrency market develops very dynamically, so tomorrow it may not behave the way it did yesterday. Therefore, the trading system, of course, is necessary, but it should be selected individually for each situation in the market. Thus, elaborating one single universal trading system "for all occasions" will not work. You need to feel the market constantly and also act in view of the specific situation.

And now I suggest considering two interesting trading systems. In fact, there are a lot of them, but we will touch upon some of the most famous ones. I will mention names of traders but do not blame me for popularizing them. We will just see what kind of trading system these successful people have chosen.

One of the most famous trading systems is called "Bill Williams Strategy." According to trader Williams, random factors determine the price, so it is impossible to predict its behavior. For this reason, this analysis does not comprise the elements of forecasting.

At the same time, we all know that the overwhelming number of analysis methods is based on the assessment of market trends. However, Williams is sure that this is the main and common mistake. Why? It is because this matter is very biased. Williams is convinced that biased interpretation of the trading system signals is the most dangerous thing for a trader.

Here are the tips of Bill Williams for using the Alligator indicator:

- Never trade against the Alligator
- If Alligator is sleeping, the fractal will be the first signal for action
- Being in position, you should track all the signals in Alligator direction and use its red line as a stop.

Here is an example of building an "Alligator" and fractals according to the strategy of Bill Williams.

By the way, I recommend using this strategy on H1 and H4 timeframes.

The second interesting strategy we will consider belongs to trader Alexander Rezvyakov. Here are its main principles:

- Trade in the direction of the global trend
- Trade with highly liquid assets
- There would be a mandatory narrow specialization in relation to traded assets
- Filter market noise and enter only during the strongest signal
- Control the expected value of profit by prompt closing unprofitable transactions and maximum possible holding of profitable positions.

Rezvyakov's strategy is unusual. For example, he suggests using two time frames: M5 and D1. On M5, it is recommended to follow only SMA to determine the average price. Another distinctive feature of this strategy is the fact that Rezvyakov proposes not to analyze the correlation of the traded instrument with foreign markets.

The main components for making a trading decision

We have considered the examples of trading strategies of some traders. Now I suggest proceeding to the *main components for making a trading decision*. Since we have analyzed the technical analysis techniques on virtually every page of this book, I propose to start from the components of fundamental analysis. Here's what you need to pay attention to when analyzing the news background of coins:

1. Statements of cryptocurrency developers
2. Statements of regulators (the People's Bank of China, the Central Bank of Singapore, the Bank of Japan, etc.)
3. Decisions of CME Group Inc. (the Chicago Mercantile Exchange Group), for example, on launching cryptocurrency futures
4. Forks (cryptocurrency divisions)
5. Important ICO projects and crowdfunding campaigns
6. Scandals associated with hacker attacks

Now let's grasp two very important points of trading that affect trading decision making: profit taking and identification of trade volume.

So, *profit taking* may occur in two variations:

1. A fixed percentage of profit is one of the easiest ways to determine target levels. You set the rate of return in percentage terms and take your profit as soon as this target is reached. This method is safer, but not as effective since you limit the growth of your profits

2. technical target level is determined through various technical analysis techniques. For example, there are methods for determining targets for many patterns of graphical analysis. The Elliott Wave Theory also clarifies the question of targets of price movements. You can also use Fibonacci extensions to define targets. And of course, you can find significant support and resistance levels and take profits near them.

Here is an approximate example of trading and profit taking on breakouts of local tops.

Finally, the second point which we should grasp: how to identify the trade volume.

The volume of your transaction depends on:

- Deposit amount
- Percent of deposit you can afford to lose in one transaction
- Market volatility

Let's learn how to calculate the trade volume. Suppose we trade a pair LTC/USD. Let's take the following example of input data for the calculation:

Your capital is $1,000

Risk as a percent of the capital is 5%

The risk in dollars is $6.85 (for example, of $137.11 price of LTC/USD pair).

The numerator is your capital multiplied by risk as a percent of capital and 0.01. The denominator is the risk in dollars multiplied by the value of one coin in dollars.

Position volume = (1000*5*0.01) / (6.85*137.11) = 50/939.20 = $0.05 (0.05323) or 0.00038 LTC.

Number 0.01 appears in the numerator to convert the value of risk as a percent of capital to a format suitable for the use in the formula of trade volume calculation.

You should also remember that different cryptocurrency pairs have different volatility. If a price change of $20 per day is normal for a pair of LTC/USD, a change in a few tenths or hundredths may be a very good indicator for others.

And now an important thing. Forget all the information about popular (or not so popular) strategies. You must form your own trading system, find your own personal strong point. One and the same trading system, which works well for one trader, may not suit another one. Therefore, if you manage to form your own set of trading rules and it brings you profit, then you can call yourself a successful trader.

Just believe in yourself. I assure you that the knowledge gained after reading this book is enough for successful sailing in the ocean called "cryptocurrency trading." However, I once again want to remind you:

> *Stay always curious and flexible; do not look for a universal trading system. Do not look for easy ways. Constantly analyze the market, learn new things and look for new approaches. Do not turn your trading rules into a kind of stagnant skeleton, change them and change yourself along with the market.*

Homework

Determine two entry and exit points using different trading strategies.

CHAPTER 14. MARKET DEPTH OR TRADING STRATEGY BASED ON MARKET DEPTH

Many experienced traders who teach beginners do not include this topic in their course. They justify this by saying you can trade without a special understanding of market depth. I agree with them to some extent but I still think that this knowledge will not harm you.

At the same time, I believe that market depth is a must-know topic for certain traders. If the exchange you choose is not particularly large, you must know the market depth. I will explain why. A large volume of transactions may move coin price on small exchanges. For example, the purchase of a large volume of Cardano can move the price of this coin up, while the sale - down. If you can analyze the market depth, you will be able to foresee this situation since you will see all the nearest pending orders for coin sale and purchase with an indication of volume.

How to assess the potential of a particular order to push the price of a coin up or down? Compare the order volume as a percentage ratio to the daily turnover of your exchange.

But first things first. What is market depth and how should we use it? The *market depth* lists all buy and sell orders for a particular coin in the exchange. Market depth displays bid and ask data. Traders, who want to buy a coin at one or another price, form a bid line, while traders who are ready to sell a coin at one or another price, form an ask line. If you place an order to buy or sell a coin, it also appears in the market depth.

Here is the example of market depth on Poloniex exchange for BTC/USDT pair.

SELL ORDERS ⇄　　　　　　　　Total: 634.30611093 BTC

Price	BTC	USDT	Sum(USDT)
6333.20739013	1.16291631	7364.99016859	7364.99016859
6333.23242000	1.26769000	8028.57540651	15393.56557510
6334.00000000	1.95870244	12406.42125496	27799.98683005
6334.65326053	1.10200000	6980.78789310	34780.77472316
6335.65417677	0.19233142	1218.54536445	35999.32008761
6336.91644999	0.00150685	9.54878255	36008.86887016
6338.08631193	0.08900000	564.08968176	36572.95855192
6338.08631194	1.67100000	10590.94222725	47163.90077917
6339.68557696	0.50000000	3169.84278848	50333.74356765
6341.47695547	1.46100000	9264.89783194	59598.64139959
6342.00000000	1.00000000	6342.00000000	65940.64139959
6342.66000000	0.00258957	16.42476206	65957.06616165
6346.59000000	0.10820000	686.70103800	66643.76719965
6346.59999999	0.75999973	4823.41428641	71467.18148606
6349.99999999	3.50000000	22224.99999996	93692.18148602
6350.00000000	0.09440749	599.48756150	94291.66904752

BUY ORDERS　　　　　　　　Total: 6468604.00887059 USDT

Price	BTC	USDT	Sum(USDT)
6333.16909974	0.00015804	1.00089404	1.00089404
6330.00000000	0.44075829	2789.99997570	2791.00086974
6329.44915977	0.00015813	1.00087580	2792.00174554
6328.33006753	0.40000000	2531.33202701	5323.33377255
6328.31371637	0.19256158	1218.59008796	6541.92386051
6327.56135000	1.27801000	8086.68668091	14628.61054141
6325.50657000	0.03145993	198.99999391	14827.61053532
6325.50000000	1.00000000	6325.50000000	21153.11053533
6325.15000000	0.02213386	139.99998458	21293.11051991
6323.79998999	0.14300000	904.30339857	22197.41391848
6323.79998998	0.52626147	3327.97227871	25525.38619719
6322.00000000	0.00457517	28.92422474	25554.31042193
6321.00000000	0.06069008	383.62199568	25937.93241761
6320.00000000	0.24000000	1516.80000000	27454.73241761
6319.66743181	3.50000000	22118.83601134	49573.56842895
6318.57108864	0.00000274	0.01731288	49573.58574183

Throttle Updates　1s ⇅　　　Order Grouping　6 decimals ⇅

Apart from market depth, I also recommend paying attention to the data of Trade history table, which, as a rule, is under market depth on the website of your exchange. All the executed orders are displayed here. Thanks to this data, you will be able to evaluate which orders were active or passive, whether large orders were executed or they were removed, etc.

TRADE HISTORY [MARKET TRADES | MY TRADES]

Date	Type	Price (USDT)	Amount (BTC)	Total (USDT)
2018-10-31 09:37:53	Buy	6333.89999997	0.15472619	980.02021483
2018-10-31 09:33:54	Buy	6333.20739016	0.11655602	738.17344723
2018-10-31 09:33:54	Buy	6333.20739000	0.40000000	2533.28295600
2018-10-31 09:33:54	Buy	6333.20738999	0.18344398	1161.78876978
2018-10-31 09:30:17	Buy	6331.11000000	0.00044697	2.82981623
2018-10-31 09:30:17	Buy	6331.11000000	0.02855440	180.78104738
2018-10-31 09:30:17	Buy	6331.10999997	0.80546367	5099.47909574
2018-10-31 09:29:59	Buy	6331.11000000	0.00100000	6.33111000
2018-10-31 09:26:42	Buy	6330.00000000	0.01779406	112.63639980
2018-10-31 09:22:29	Buy	6330.00000000	0.01882291	119.14902030
2018-10-31 09:22:29	Buy	6330.00000000	0.03992490	252.72461700
2018-10-31 09:22:28	Buy	6330.00000000	0.01072500	67.88925000
2018-10-31 09:22:27	Buy	6330.00000000	0.00862559	54.59998470
2018-10-31 09:22:27	Buy	6330.00000000	0.01836522	116.25184260
2018-10-31 09:21:45	Buy	6330.00000000	0.01592680	100.81664400
2018-10-31 09:21:44	Buy	6330.00000000	0.01561888	98.86751040

Now let's move on to the strategy of trading using market depth. In fact, this strategy is as simple as ABC.

How do I recommend entering the market so that your order is more likely to be executed? You need to join the large market players. Place your order before another large order you find in the market depth.

Suppose you found an order with very large volume for EOS sale in market depth. You place your order to sell this coin at the same price as a big player did. A big order from a player with large volume can move the price in his direction, so your order will be executed also. We make a bet on it.

Thanks to market depth, you can also see a possible reversal. For example, the market goes down, but you see the orders with large volume placed for purchase in market depth. In such a situation it is possible that these orders will manage to stop the market from falling and give it a boost.

Always try to analyze the market depth carefully, so you can understand how far the price can go down or up.

But do not forget there are both active and passive orders. No one can guarantee that a big player you follow will not cancel his order. After all, many large orders are placed only to scare less experienced players.

You should also understand that it is important not to be greedy in this strategy. You should take your profit immediately, even if in small parts. A large order can shift the price in one direction or another, but we do not know how big this shift will be, so it is important to take your profit on time.

At the same time, you need to understand there are psychological lines and levels. As a rule, large orders are placed at certain psychological levels. First, find a large order in the market depth and then look where it is on the chart. A strong level is most likely to stay within this price range.

In a word, the analysis of market depth is not an obligatory component of a successful trader, but knowledge of this tool can become a kind of joker in your deck of cards, confirming that the market is moving the same way you forecasted.

Therefore, in order to get a qualitative result of your forecasts, you should combine technical analysis with market depth data on your exchange. Sometimes market depth can be informative and it may help you not only make a high-quality analysis but also find the most successful entry and exit points.

CHAPTER 15.
FUNDAMENTAL ANALYSIS

To forecast the price movement of traded cryptocurrency, a trader has two main methods: fundamental and technical analysis. Whereas the technical analysis, which we have already analyzed in detail, is the cryptocurrency value forecast based on charts, the fundamental analysis is based on economic, political and social factors, i.e. on analysis of all the available information about a particular coin. An analyst is looking for a logical chain of links that may lead to certain consequences.

Technical analysis may help forecast the currency value in the short term, while fundamental analysis focuses on the long term. Therefore, fundamental analysis is not about price, it is about all the factors that influence its movement. Fundamental analysis requires an in-depth study of all the facts, including those that affect the currency value over a long period of time — a week, a month, or several months. In other words, fundamental analysis is the study of what is not yet on the chart but what will eventually become the subject of technical analysis.

If you think that fundamental analysis is much simpler than the technical one, I will have to disagree with you. Finding a causal relationship between price and a bulk of news is not easy at all.

If you ask which of the two methods of analysis is more effective, then I will answer both of them. A professional trader is a participant in the financial market who is able to use all the tools of analysis.

Fundamental analysis techniques were first used in the American traditional market, and its founders are considered to be two American financiers - Benjamin Graham and David Dodd, who published the book "Security Analysis" in 1934. It is on this work that the analysts of all financial markets, using the fundamental analysis, still rely.

Fundamental analysis is based on several theses:

1. Price of any asset changes because of certain reasons (for example, in trading we must look for an imbalance between the market price and real value)
2. Reasons for the price change can be detected through a detailed study of the facts which concern a particular asset
3. Every fact entails certain consequences that affect an asset price
4. If you know all the facts and make correct logical conclusions, you can predict what will happen to an asset in the future.

So, if you decide to conduct the fundamental analysis, you need the following elements:

- Market regulation news
- Political and economic events (meetings of the world leaders to discuss the regulation and development of the cryptocurrency market; state programs and measures on the elaboration of corresponding legislation within the country, etc.)
- News of companies involved in cryptocurrency business (forks, integration with the real economy sector, an update of the company's roadmap, etc.)
- Press conferences of the actors who influence the market

Now let's identify all those sources of information that we most often use for fundamental analysis in cryptocurrency trading:

- Information about cryptocurrency itself (sites of developers, coinmarketcap.com and similar resources, Twitter, Reddit, Telegram channels, etc.)
- Bloomberg - one of the leading providers of financial information for professional participants in financial markets
- CNBC - American cable and satellite business news channel
- Reuters - one of the world's largest international news and financial news agencies

In addition, there is also so-called "off-the-record" information, for example, insider data. But it must be checked very carefully.

In short, you need to use a large number of different resources to conduct a fundamental analysis of the cryptocurrency market. However, do not forget that you cannot boil the ocean. You will not be able to take into account all the information at once, therefore I suggest filtering sources.

Let me explain. For example, I know many fellow traders who monitor more than 40 Telegram channels about cryptocurrency. Over time, they have got lost in information and now they are not able to separate main information from secondary, not to mention fakes.

Judging from my personal experience, I should say that a large amount of news for analysis is bad, but a small amount of news for analysis is also bad. What should we do then? Find the minimum number of quality sources for analyzing news. If you spend too much time reading the news, and then spend a lot of time on technical analysis, you may start to hate trading in half a year. Therefore, look for the optimal amount of resources to get the needed information for fundamental analysis.

It may seem that everything is simple: just read the news and analyze it. However, the problem of the cryptocurrency market lies in the fact that it is very young and remains unregulated, which means it is a little bit "wild" and can be manipulated. That is why we do not have an information field that can be 100% trusted. Sometimes we cannot determine whether the information we have found out about a project is true or a manipulation from the concerned party. Believe me, there are many concerned parties in the cryptocurrency market.

For instance, when one of the world's largest news agencies publishes a certain piece of news making many investors "dump" a certain cryptocurrency, and later this agency says "Sorry, we mixed something up", the question arises: was it a mistake?

Therefore, two psychological states of fear always prevail in the cryptocurrency market: one fear is that you may miss the opportunity of making money, while the second one is uncertainty: won't it all go belly up now? These two emotions always compete, and big players and concerned parties constantly incite them. Therefore, it is difficult for us to assemble a whole picture like a puzzle from many components of fundamental analysis and to make a final conclusion on the direction of the cryptocurrency movement.

But let's look at the cryptocurrency market on the other side, which, on the contrary, demonstrates the advantages of being "wild" and easily manipulated. Nowadays there are practically no professional participants in the cryptocurrency market. Most market players are private investors.

What is the difference between the "wild" cryptocurrency market and other traditional markets?

- Pumps/dumps (artificially increase or decrease in the coin value)
- High volatility
- Vibrant movement of the crowd

On the one hand, all these factors are a kind of advantage as they make our process of making money much easier. However, you need to understand that the impact of these factors will end sooner or later. Therefore, we'll benefit from these advantages while we have such an opportunity)

And finally, here are some sites and services I recommend bookmarking on your computer:

www.tradingview.com is a social network (we have already discussed it before), where various traders share their trading ideas; other participants have the opportunity not only to monitor how the traders' forecasts work but also to "draw" on their charts

www.coinmarketcap.com allows monitoring dynamics of cryptocurrency market

www.worldcoinindex.com is a service that allows tracking statistics on coins. Here you can see the dynamics of coin development even, for example, for a year period

www.coinigy.com allows you to unite in one place many exchanges on which you can trade simultaneously

www.coinchecup.com allows getting even more information on coins and the dynamics of their development

www.3commas.io helps to trade on exchanges automatically

www.iconomi.net helps to find out about ICOs

www.coinmarketcal.com is a calendar of coin news

I will not name specific news sites for getting information on the cryptocurrency market. It's a very subjective matter as some traders believe the news site which others consider to be crap. The choice is yours.

Remember one thing: in order to conduct a qualitative fundamental analysis, first make up your mind on the sources of information. Make a list of specific sites you trust. If you trade within the day, you will need news feeds that provide real-time information. If you focus on long-term trading, reading news reviews in the evenings will be enough for you.

Fundamental indicators for coin analysis

We have discussed, without going into details, the information and resources for fundamental analysis, but now let's take a closer look at the fundamental indicators we should assess if you have already chosen a particular cryptocurrency you want to speculate.

Demand for the cryptocurrency. You need to understand who and why there is need this or that cryptocurrency. Cryptocurrency community participants are interested in the coins that can be useful to the market itself or can integrate into the economy.

Each cryptocurrency has its purpose. Some are intended for transfer of value, other may help build a certain business, while others are designed for storing huge databases. Each cryptocurrency is tailored to reach certain goals, so it is obvious that every coin cannot be suitable for every person. Nowadays there are about 2,000 different types of cryptocurrency. Each of them offers some kind of value. But remember that value is not equal to price. The market may be too enthusiastic or too skeptical about a particular coin. Our goal is to catch the moment when there is a discrepancy between real value and market price.

Methods of mining or receiving cryptocurrency. You need to estimate how many people may have this currency in the future and, accordingly, how many people will use it. For example, we understand that Bitcoin mining is not cheap as you have to buy special equipment and pay electricity bills. Since this process is permanent, the Bitcoin miners are unlikely to sell it at a loss. They will form a certain price and will not sell cheaper.

Number of coins which already exist and pending release. If you evaluate this factor in the coin of your choice, you can understand its potential relevance in the future. It is not a secret to anyone that a limited amount of a particular coin increases its value, while unlimited emission, on the contrary, can devalue the currency, especially if it is not so popular. For example, if you wonder why XRP is much cheaper than Bitcoin, just compare the amount of both coins in circulation.

The current position of the cryptocurrency in the market. This fundamental indicator is estimated by a number of economic factors. The current position of coin affects its future. For example, cryptocurrency with a billion-dollar capitalization has more prospects than an asset with a capitalization of $10,000. Here you have a simple example: four unknown guys working in some kind of God-forgotten garage have more chances to increase their capital thousand-fold compared with the world-famous Google.

Trading volume. This indicator shows the number of people interested in cryptocurrency. Moreover, you should distinguish between traders and long-term investors. The domination of traders points to the value of the coin as a momentary speculative tool, while the prevalence of investors indicates its prospects in the future.

Indicators of price growth. The price can demonstrate not just an increase or decrease in the market value of a coin, but also an increase or decrease in the people interested in it.

The position of cryptocurrency in the traditional market. By analyzing this aspect, you will be able to understand the further relevance of a coin outside the cryptocurrency market. Here it is necessary to use the facts concerning the policy of states towards a coin. For example, permissions, bans, use in a particular industry and so on.

Information about the developer. Find out who stands for a coin and how these people can contribute to its development.

Analysis of the current attitudes of users. We are interested in the attitude of coin users to its prospects.

These are all the main fundamental indicators for coin analysis. However, I want to emphasize there may be many more facts to research. This list may be different for each particular coin, and your task, as an analyst, is to collect as many facts about a particular cryptocurrency as possible.

Now I will present an unsophisticated fundamental analysis strategy, which I call "Trading using the news." It is based on the release of important economic, political or other news, which the cryptocurrency, as a rule, is very sensitive to.

I would divide all news into planned and unplanned ones. The planned news are released according to the news calendar, while unplanned occur spontaneously, so it is very difficult to base your work on such news. So, if you know that a positive piece of news about certain coin will be released on a particular day, you should place an order to buy it. If the news is good, the price of your coin will soar and you will manage to make money on it.

In fact, trading using news should not be underestimated. A lot of large investors in the cryptocurrency market spend a lot of money on access to news services to find out information a little bit earlier than other market participants.

You may have encountered such a situation: you read important news about a coin, go to the exchange and see a very active movement is taking place there for a while already. You join this movement by placing your buy order, but what a bad luck, the market already starts to decline. What happened? The fact is that the information that was fresh news for you was no longer such for market makers or large sharks of the market. They stood at the very beginning of the upward wave of coin price because of this news, while you jump in when they began to close positions. Whom do you think these sharks sell their coins at the last moment? They sell them to you. That is, without knowing it, you became one of those traders "milked" by big players.

Pros and cons of fundamental analysis

The first thing you need to remember is that fundamental analysis is not a cure-all. Despite the fact that it can break technical analysis by reversing the trend, the fundamental analysis should be used along with technical analysis.

Fundamental analysis is used for both investing and trading. It fits investing even better since with its help we can understand which coins we should add to our investment portfolio and which ones we should remove. Using fundamental analysis in short-term trading, we can understand what news will make coin shoot upwards.

Fundamental analysis allows us to get a general notion of the cryptocurrency market and to focus on it. It improves the quality of your forecast, but by itself is not able to answer the main question: buy or sell. It is an auxiliary tool. It is invaluable for teaching us to distinguish between reliable currencies and fraudulent ones.

Fundamental analysis of cryptocurrency is a reliable tool for making long-term forecasts. Despite the diversity of information for analysis, it is difficult to miss the most important, significant facts. Most information needed for basic research is on open access (from economic indicators to community activity indicators), so the main array of information is always at the disposal of an analyst. But do not forget that fundamental analysis works only for long-term forecasting, i.e., it will not show you the entry or exit points. For short-term "guessing", you need to apply technical analysis.

Now let's talk about the shortcomings of fundamental analysis.

The need to collect all the information about cryptocurrency, reported in different sources and at different times, is one of the main drawbacks of fundamental analysis. This makes fundamental analysis very limitedly applicable for a beginner. So, in practice, it is not so easy to establish cause-and-effect relations as it may seem at first glance. For example, I hope you know that EOS is the main competitor of Ethereum. What impact should it have on Ethereum? Quite bad, but on the other hand, we remember the rule "Price takes into account everything." Therefore, when the EOS price grows, the Ethereum does not fall necessarily.

But let's ask ourselves one more question: do any analyses providing 100% forecast of the cryptocurrency market behavior exist? The answer to this question is unequivocal: they do not exist, unless you are Nostradamus, of course. The cryptocurrency market is so volatile it is impossible to predict 100%.

If you are still convinced that you make forecasts with a 100% guarantee, I will prove how any of your forecasts can turn from a 100% guarantee into a complete fiasco. To do this, I will list some factors that trigger changes in the cryptocurrency market:

- Government regulatory bodies
- Supply and demand in the market
- Involvement of the world's population
- Fake news
- News from "manipulators"
- Compliance with the roadmap of cryptocurrency projects
- Hacker attacks and related hazards

However, fortunately, all these factors most often influence a coin price as an exception rather than a rule. Therefore, all the tools for analyzing cryptocurrency remain relevant. Each trader forms their own personal set of tools which allows making the most accurate possible forecast.

However, this happens through trial and error over a long period of fruitful work.

Cryptocurrency market regulation: pros and cons

The appearance of regulatory bodies in the cryptocurrency market can affect its fundamental development, so I decided to share my opinion on this issue.

My stance on this matter is very clear: the regulators in the cryptocurrency market are needed. Cryptocurrency regulation is important for the development of the economy and the financial sector. Let's list the main and obvious reasons why a regulator is good:

- Manipulations will decrease
- Introduction of rules and arrival of professional participants will trigger real market growth
- Anonymity will disappear (although this factor can be both positive and negative). To date, there are three cryptocurrencies that provide genuine anonymity: Zcash, Dash and Monero. In fact, they are incompatible with regulators so they are likely to be the first to suffer in the future.

Apart from the bright task of regulators to protect market participants from the illegal actions of fraudsters, they can also have a vague or unusual task for us: to collect taxes from market participants.

And now let me highlight my personal 4 pros and 4 cons of cryptocurrency market regulation.

Pros:

1. Appearance of worthy token projects
2. The growth of market capitalization
3. Security of funds
4. The appearance of official regulated cryptocurrency exchanges

Cons:

1. Scam of individual tokens, which are created for mere collecting money or making a financial pyramid
2. First cryptocurrency enthusiasts may leave the market
3. Imposition of a tax burden
4. Lower market volatility

Speaking in favor of regulators, I also want to remind you that not a single financial market had attracted trillions of dollars until regulation appeared on it. In addition, the cryptocurrency market regulation is a way to capitalize up to $20 trillion or more. I suppose this will happen not due to the rise in Bitcoin hike but thanks to the appearance of new types of cryptocurrency.

By the way, the growth and development of the cryptocurrency market will occur not only because of the introduction of rules but also due to the start of so-called "securitization." What is it? It means the attraction of funding to the market through the creation of new tools provided with cryptocurrency. In other words, an unlimited number of derivatives will appear on the market.

To date, we've witnessed the first examples of securitization:

- Futures contracts
- Option contracts
- CFD instruments (Contract For Difference) - an arrangement made in futures contract whereby differences in a settlement are made through cash payments.

Time will tell whether the regulatory bodies will appear in the cryptocurrency market or not. But do not forget that cryptocurrency itself is just a security. The regulators create rules around it, while manipulators spread panic and trigger market fall.

Now we need to pay attention not to future regulators, but to those organizations that already fulfill their functions to some extent:

- SEC - United States Securities and Exchange Commission (this organization could strictly dictate its rules in the market in the future)
- JFSA - Japan's financial regulator
- The Fed - United States Central Bank
- NBK – People's Bank of China;
- ECB - Central Bank of the EU.

Homework

1) Make a fundamental analysis of the cryptocurrency market for the past month. Find the most important news that influenced the overall market dynamics

2) Identify the fake news that became a tool for manipulating the cryptocurrency market.

CHAPTER 16. RISK AND MONEY MANAGEMENT

W e can all admit that any investment in our life is fraught with risk, and the greater the expected profit is, the greater is the risk. We always fear that the invested money may not pay off at all or will pay off partially without bringing substantial profit.

Trading on a cryptocurrency exchange is also impossible to do without risk. If you want to become a successful trader, you need to know not only the basics of technical and fundamental analysis but also those of risk and capital management. Therefore, let's understand why heightened risks emerge and how to minimize them.

Before you open a position, you always need to remember that profit is proportional to risk. Everything depends on the tactics of your trade. Some are inclined to trade for the long-term, while others prefer to trade more aggressively within the day. In any case, risk should not exceed 10% of the monthly capital for aggressive trading and 5% for long-term trading.

My advice can be expressed mathematically:

$P = k1*R$, where P is profit, $k1$ is a coefficient of trader's experience (the more professional the trader is, the higher is the coefficient) and R is a risk.

Factors that scale up your trading risks

Now let's fetch out some factors that may scale up your trading risks.

One of the reasons why most traders lose their money is the fact that they **care most about an entry point and think about leaving the position at the last second**. It is strange as it is the right exit point that determines our income or loss. Often most of our entry points fall within the profitability zone, but we still lose money due to the lack of correct exit strategy. This happens for two reasons: we remain in a position for too long, waiting for an even greater increase in profit, and as a result, the price reverses. Or we close too quickly, afraid to lose the small profits we have gained.

How to avoid such a risk? You should plan an exit point before you open a position.

The absence of a trading strategy. Newcomers often make this error as they do not understand that trading in the cryptocurrency market without a clear trading plan is equal to suicide. Professional traders, on the contrary, take a very balanced approach to the elaboration of a trading strategy, which at the same time should be flexible enough to adapt to certain market situations. An important factor in this strategy is its clear implementation. If you do not follow your strategy, then what is the use of it?

We have already discussed trading strategies, and you can find more information about how to keep track of all your transactions in the *Trader's Diary* section. Apart from notes on entry and exit points and other technical data, you can leave in a diary your "psycho-emotional" notes that will help you to trade successfully.

In fact, the trading strategy also helps a trader to relieve emotional distress. You will have no doubts or concerns when making a particular trading decision as the full algorithm of actions will be spelled out in your strategy, which you must follow.

Another risk is **wrong thinking**. I also call this risk "Inflated expectations." Some traders come to the cryptocurrency market with a clear conviction they can make money here quickly and without any particular understanding of the market. But later, due to wrong decisions, these people start to lose their capital. In order to not repeat their mistake, you should not enter the market without having studied its peculiarities. Without the necessary knowledge of technical and fundamental analysis, your risk of losing your capital increases greatly. However, in my opinion, the fact you are now holding this book in your hands already says you a have a sound approach towards studying the market.

One of the worst traits of character that raises your risks sky-high is your **emotions**. It is impossible to turn them off completely, but you still have to learn how to manage them. Panic and fear, which can sometimes seize you, will lead to the devastation of the investment portfolio. Your trade should be guided by your logic, not emotions. We will talk about the psychology of trading in more detail at the end of the book.

Wrong choice of traded coin or cryptocurrency exchange. Many traders do not bother to pay enough attention to finding good coins and good exchange. For example, some traders work on exchanges with very high fees, without thinking it will be more efficient to register on one of the top exchanges. Moreover, working on a little-known stock exchange, you risk joining the ranks of non-achievers who lose all their money because of the fraudulent tricks of the exchange developers. Examine all the nuances of your stock exchange before you deposit money into your trading account. You should be very scrupulous about choosing an exchange.

Therefore, correct all the nuances and start to move towards success before your money disappears in the bottomless "pocket" of the exchange.

Money management

A professional trader should not only be able to analyze the market and minimize risks but also manage their capital in a way that profits always exceed losses. Capital management includes a number of important factors: smart formation of the investment portfolio, estimation of the investments in a coin, correct ratio between risk and profit, etc. Therefore, if you think that choosing the right trading strategy is much more important than the ability to manage your capital correctly, you are on a false path. If you want to stay in the trading world of for long, you should master capital management.

So, the cornerstone of money management is the ability to protect the available capital, not to increase the profit. Let's now discuss a number of techniques for efficient capital management.

Determine the optimal risk for a position

Roughly speaking, you have to decide what amount of money you are willing to sacrifice in this or that transaction. But as I said earlier, I do not recommend having a risk exceeding 10% in one trade. Although sometimes the market develops in such a way you will have to show flexibility and change this figure. In most cases, stay true to this rule.

Diversify

Diversification is not only a method of capital management; it is also a method of protecting capital. This rule works on the principle "Don't put all your eggs in one basket." Your investment portfolio should not contain only Bitcoin or only Ethereum. It's better to distribute the capital among several coins. Such an approach will allow you to stay afloat and continue to make money, even if one of your coins fizzles out.

Although there is no single answer to the question of the right extent of capital diversification, I will give you advice based on my personal experience: do not invest more than 30% of your capital in one coin. This rule will allow you to protect yourself from excessive investment in one currency and to make sure that possible losses from one failed transaction do not ruin you, but are offset by profits from others.

Use protective stop orders

Using a stop order, you protect your capital from unwanted price movements. In other words, this technique implies a clear prediction of how long you are ready to stay in an unprofitable position. However, it's not so easy because the indication of the level at which the stop order should be placed is a real art. The more volatile the market is, the farther from the current level of prices you should place a stop loss order. At the same time, you should stick to a certain balance, because if you place a stop order too close to the price level, wanting to minimize losses almost to zero, your position could be eliminated amid short-term price fluctuations (in this case you need to increase percentage of stop order, and accordingly that of profit). If you place a stop order around 8%, that means your profit should be 30-40%.

Conversely, if you place a stop order too far from the current price, you risk losing a lot. Therefore, the art of trading lies in the ability to find the "golden mean".

It is worth noting that so-called "**trailing" stops** also exist in the market. This limiter follows the price at a specified distance. It is also called a "sliding stop." It is not fixed at a certain level so it moves first to the breakeven zone, and then to the profit zone.

Let's explain in more detail how the trailing stop works. Suppose you have opened a position on BTC/USDT cryptocurrency pair. You understand that if the price reverses 30 points down, you will need to close the position. It is at this level that you set the trailing stop. If the price starts moving upwards by more than 30 points, then your trailing stop will follow the price at the distance you specify. Therefore, if the trailing stop goes into the profitability zone and the price reverses down, you will still close your position in profit.

The disadvantage of this kind of stop-loss order is that random market fluctuations can knock it out if it is placed at a short distance from the price. At the same time, do not forget that it begins to work only when the price reaches a predetermined profit value, and until then your position remains without a stop. That is why I recommend placing stop loss first. You can do it at the same level as the trailing stop.

By the way, sometimes determination of level for setting a stop loss can forbid opening a position at all. For example, during the analysis, you can understand that a stop loss will be so far from the entry point that in case of successful trade your profit will be much smaller, whereas, in the case of unsuccessful one, the loss will be very high. In this case, it is better to abandon the transaction.

I must also admit that many traders do not use stop-loss orders in their trading at all, but their stance is not correct in terms of classical trading as in case of a drawdown of a coin on which you did not want to fix a loss, you turn from a trader into a long-term investor. It is better to fix a small loss than to wait until your asset rises from the bottom of the drawdown since the drawdown can last long.

However, it's up to you to decide whether you should place a stop order or not. If it is more comfortable for you to trade without it, then do so, but do not forget to control your losses in some other way.

Track important economic news

It is better if all your positions are closed, i.e., that you are out of the market at the time of the release of important news. The price may often respond to the news in a unpredictable way on the "wild" cryptocurrency market. In order to avoid unforeseen situations, track the calendar of economic planned events, the result of which is not known in advance.

Profit-to-loss ratio

According to some statistics, 40% of traders' transactions are profitable. You will ask yourself: how then do they earn money if more than half of their transactions are unprofitable? And here we come to the problem of profit-to-loss ratio.

Thus, we should determine the rate of profit for each transaction, which must be balanced with potential losses if the market moves in an undesirable direction. Usually, this ratio should be 3:1, that is the potential profit should be at least three times greater than the potential loss. Otherwise, you should give up the deal. For example, if the risk is 10%, the profit should reach at least 30%.

Trade, using several strategies for one coin

We have repeatedly touched upon the topic that sometimes traders lose their capital due to the fact they close a position too early, fearing not to have time to take their profit before the price reversal. How should you act in such a case? My answer is that you can try to trade, using two different strategies for one coin. Opening diverse positions is a win-win strategy since trading simultaneously on two positions may increase your chances of making a profit.

For example, there is an upward trend in the market. You open two positions: you leave the first one after the first signal of a possible price reversal while keeping the second one open to the point of your expected profit.

The one who trades aggressively makes a large profit, but this will continue only as long as the market moves in the desired direction. A conservative trader does not make much money but does not fall too low either.

Remember that the bigger growth a coin price has demonstrated in a short period of time, the less percentage of capital you should invest in a deal. After all, this signals that a coin is "running hot" and the price reversal is already closed. And the opposite situation: the more a coin values drops, the more you need to find the right entry points to it. But do not forget we are talking only about top coins. I do not take shitcoins into account.

How to overcome drawdown

Given the fact that a very dynamic and prolonged downtrend has started in the cryptocurrency market in 2018, many traders found themselves in a not very pleasant situation called a *drawdown*. What is drawdown and how do you cope with it?

Drawdown is the amount by which your trading deposit decreases. Sometimes the drawdown magnitude can even reach the value of the deposit itself. This magnitude should be measured as a percentage of the size of your investment portfolio, because it does not matter how much it is in USD or EUR, it is important what percentage of your deposit "touched the bottom." You must agree that there is a difference in the drawdown of $5,000 with a deposit of $10,000 and the same drawdown of $5,000 with a deposit of $ 100,000.

Why are traders who went into a drawdown called long-term investors? Because their positions on a particular coin remain open. Therefore, their transactions are in a floating state and can both decrease and increase.

But there is also fixed drawdown when a trader has closed all losing positions in the red.

How to overcome both types of drawdown? There are two ways: skillful money management under existing positions and an opening of new ones.

The most difficult thing is to overcome a fixed drawdown, since your loss is visible not only on the computer monitor, you feel it in your pocket, in the real numbers of the investment portfolio. There are two ways to solve the problem: aggressive and conservative. The **aggressive one means** you should open a position in double volume. That is, you open a new position in double volume per every unprofitable position. If it turns out to be profitable, you will break even; but if it is unprofitable, then you will fall even lower.

Those, who consider an aggressive approach to be risky can use a more relaxed option: **averaging a position**. To overcome drawdown, you need to build up the unprofitable position. You may say it defies common sense, but in any case, it helps to cope with the drawdown, since you average a coin price at which you have opened a loss-making position, making it more profitable.

I'll cite an example. Suppose you purchased 1,000 Litecoins at $100 for a coin. However, your positive forecast did not work and the price began to fall down and stopped at around $70. You need to purchase another 1,000 coins at a new price of $ 70. Thus, you will have 2,000 coins at a price of $85 for a coin (100 + 70) / 2 = 85). If the price of this coin goes up again, you will have a lot of coins at a profitable purchase price.

In a word, you cannot trade without risks, which means mistakes. He who makes no mistakes does nothing (or is delusional). I am sure there is no trader in this world, who has not experienced risks and has not made mistakes. Mistakes are given to us to learn from them. This book was also created, among other things, to show you where all the "rakes" are hidden and teach you to avoid them or at least minimize the number of bumps on your forehead.

CHAPTER 17. TRADER'S DIARY

Discipline is no less important for a successful trader than technical and fundamental analysis, trading strategy or risk management. Traders often lose their capital as they do not know how to control their own emotions. It is emotion that can ruin your deals. It is difficult to learn how to control them, especially when you realize that your forecast will not hit the target and the price goes in the opposite direction. At this point, you are most likely to make impulsive decisions.

Nevertheless, there is light at the end of the tunnel. A trader's diary will help you to stay disciplined and not succumb to your emotions. It is an essential attribute of a successful trader. You should write down all the information about open positions in this diary. In this way, you will be able to analyze the gained experience and make the necessary conclusions.

Some traders underestimate the need for keeping a diary, claiming they keep all the information about deals in their heads. However, such a stance is the first step towards losses. A diary helps to analyze all transactions and, therefore, helps to learn from your mistakes. Those traders, who do not analyze and do not learn from their mistakes will repeat them in the future.

A trader's diary can help analyze each position, the reasons for its opening, etc. At the same time, thanks to the diary, you will be protected from spontaneous decisions as you can look into the diary and remember why you opened this or that position and when it should be closed.

There is no definite standard or template of a trader's diary. You can keep it in any form convenient to you. The main thing is that it should contain the information about all your positions. Write down notes about each position: what was a signal for its opening, the entry price, and the predicted exit. At the same time, during each transaction, describe your feelings, assumptions and other notes that will contain emotional evaluations, not numbers. Later, all these records will help you remember the sequence of actions of a successful transaction you will want to repeat as well as the algorithm of a loss-making trade, which must be avoided.

Although there is no clear trader's diary template, as I said earlier, I can show you my example of this transaction log. If you find it useful, you may use it for your trading.

Link on the diary - http://bit.ly/alans-trade-diary

Let's imagine we make the first deal and start to keep this trader's diary. For example, you open a Bitcoin chart and notice a confident upward price movement. We write this in the first cell of the table. Then we indicate the strength of the coin price movement. In the next cell called "Commentary", we describe our actions, for example, "Buy only" or "Look for take profit points." Next, we describe the direction and strength of oscillators. Then we enter all the data of technical analysis: Japanese candlesticks, resistance and support levels, Fibonacci lines. Next, go to the news. If you know some news about the acquired coin - write it in the table. Finally, we leave a commentary on the news and, of course, the result is whether we should buy or sell the coin.

According to this principle, you write down all the data on each timeframe: week, day, 4 hours and 1 hour.

And there is another table in which I give an example of how to enter the data on purchased coins. It is in the same file below the first table.

If keeping a table is not a version of diary which suits you, you can take an ordinary notebook for writing down all the information about your deals: entry and exit points, comments on them and conclusions (why you get a particular result).

No matter what you use – table or notebook - leave abundant comments on each deal. Why is this important? First, while describing your actions, you will find more answers to various questions. Second, you can view and analyze a specific sequence of actions that led to a right or wrong decision.

In general, a trader's diary will help you not only keep track of trades but also see your own weak points and enforce the strong ones. A diary will help you figure out whether your trading strategy works well or not.

How to organize your work day

To reach top performance, a trader needs to organize their workday correctly. Improper organization of working hours may entail losses in transactions. Therefore, let's learn how to organize your workflow properly.

Since cryptocurrency exchanges operate around the clock, you can choose any time convenient for you to check your open positions. Sometimes even one news item can affect the coin price movement, so you should check the market situation, especially your deals, every day. After that, I recommend devoting 1-2 hours to the study of coins which may be interesting for trade. Some use technical analysis for such purposes, others resort to fundamental analysis, but no matter what path you choose, the result should be the same: opening of interesting positions. In addition, I recommend making notes on what points you should pay attention to the next day.

However, I do not advise you to follow the charts too often. There's no need to go to Tradingview every hour and check the forecast. Such convulsive and nervous monitoring of the price can lead to mistakes, and, moreover, it will wear you down quickly. Do not turn your open deal into a price tracking mania. To avoid this situation, try to choose large timeframes (4H or 1D). At such time intervals, your forecast will need more time to hit the target.

It's up to you to decide how many hours a day you will devote to trading. If you prefer scalping, you will need a lot of time for trading (although you can reduce this time by using the algorithmic trading), but if you are not going to devote yourself to this profession completely - no problem, you can trade for no more than 2 hours a day. You can solve all major trading issues in a few hours and enjoy life the rest of the time.

That is why the correct and simple organization of a work day can save time and help avoid emotional decisions and undesirable financial losses.

CHAPTER 18. PSYCHOLOGY OF TRADING

We all understand that emotions are an integral part of a person. It is clear that we cannot pause them during an unexpected situation in the cryptocurrency market, but we can learn to control them. At least it's worth trying because emotions are a guaranteed component of your failure in cryptocurrency trading. Your psychological state at the time of trading may affect your account. You need to know the enemy by sight, so you should be able to identify unnecessary emotions and nip them in the bud because later it will be difficult to keep your head cool during an unforeseen price reversal.

Accept that you cannot control the behavior of the market, but you can learn to control your attitude towards it, your emotions.

Trading, like any other profession, requires a whole set of certain psychological qualities from you. These qualities don't have to be be innate, you can adopt them.

So what qualities should trader have to be successful?

The first and most important is intellect. **IQ** of a successful trader cannot be below average. A lot of sophisticated tools for simplification of trading could be invented, for example, trading robots. However, it is impossible to trade without your own mental abilities. Even the most cutting-edge trading robots do not know how to independently adapt to a certain market situation.

At the same time, a **trader should have an analytical mindset** as trading is not about "buy-sell" transactions – it's about the analysis of how and when a particular transaction should be carried out.

Self-discipline is another important trait of a successful trader, which we have already discussed. You will get a stable profitable result only if you stick to your trading strategy and do not make impulsive trading decisions.

Purposefulness and patience. A successful trader treats short-term failures not as a punishment of the Lord but as a temporary stage on the path towards success. Patience helps to augment your capital slowly but steadily.

Power of thought and affirmations

How powerful are our thoughts? Is there a possibility of absolute transformation of thoughts into real events? I am SURE of it! Of course, skeptics will say it is nonsense and our thoughts are just a flight of imagination. However, I believe that any thoughts project our present and future. Thoughts are not the result of events, but the first tool for creating these events. Thoughts fly away into the space of options, but supported by the strength of our faith (or even fear) return with the result we expect and not necessarily the one we want. So, you are afraid of something = expect and receive; confidently go to the goal and have strong faith = want and receive.

Faith is not just a fluctuation of air, it is the energy. You cannot see or hear it, but it works!

The Bible says that if we have faith at least the size of a mustard seed and say to a mountain, "Move from here to there," it will move. One of my favorite authors also writes "Fantasy does not exist as such. Any fiction is already a reality", and also "Your thoughts always come back to you like a boomerang."

We get what we choose! Our freedom lies in our freedom of choice. And we make this choice in our thoughts...

Therefore, strange as it may sound, I believe that people can control their reality. A confident thought about getting the desired result brings your goal closer, and vice versa - the thought with doubt pushes it away. The Universe perceives doubt as a denial. If you doubt, then you shout to the Universe: "I will not succeed!" The response is almost immediate: you succeed in nothing.

You may ask why I let you into the secret rooms of my worldview and what bearing it has on trading. It has a direct bearing! A trader who believes in a positive result can be successful. From the moment you open a position till the moment you take profit, you should not be ambivalent about your choice, thinking your forecast may go to waste and you will knock down your entire deposit.

Just think what thoughts you send into space while opening a position. If you put more doubts than faith in your deals, the more likely you are to get a bad result.

How to become more confident in order to open a position with the right thoughts? There are many options, but if we are talking about psychology, one of them is autogenic training. It sounds difficult, but it is easy to use. The best example of this training is a girl who stands in the morning in front of a mirror and repeats like a spell: "I am beautiful and happy!"

It is a kind of psychological training. If it provokes your skepticism or even laughter, then know that many athletes often use such training in the preparation for competitions. This method increases their confidence in victory. The essence of the training is the repetition of certain affirmations. You declare the desired result not in the future tense, but in the present as if you already gained it. If you are struggling with shyness, you should not repeat "I want to be confident", but the statement "I am sure." Thus, you deceive your mind, letting it believe that your desire is a fait accompli.

Why does a trader need auto-training?

Most newbies make the biggest mistakes in trading because of fear. It is the fear of losing capital. And the paradox is that the less money you have, the more fear you have. You can say no to fear, including with the help of autogenic training. Try to convince your mind that you have nothing to fear. Your affirmation may sound "I make profitable deals" or choose for yourself any statement alike.

I want to warn you that I do not encourage you to trade based only on the right thoughts, unshakable faith, and psychological affirmations. Each of you should understand that first comes theoretical knowledge (technical analysis, fundamental analysis), and then everything is supported by the right way of thinking. Trading is a serious business that requires profound knowledge and experience, not just hopes for good luck.

CONCLUSION

Dear reader, I am not one of those writers who outlines their content without worrying whether it will stick in the minds of their readers and whether they will be able to take advantage of it. At the same time, I understand that all of you are different. Some will find this book a complicated science about the incomprehensible phenomenon called "trading". It is also possible that there are some people who already have certain experience in this field and, therefore, the book is not helpful for them. In any case, I have high hopes that each of you will be able to pick up useful information as my book is not only theory of technical or fundamental analysis, capital and risk management, it also includes my arguments, my experience and my personal charts that speak better than any words.

At the same time, I want to give you the final instructions on the path to your successful transactions (and I believe you will have more than enough of them).

First of all, do not forget that **cryptocurrency trading is full of paradoxes**. The curve of research here is not linear but, on the contrary, it is a labyrinth where you can get lost. Due to the fact that the cryptocurrency market is young, wild and unpredictable, there are no standard identical trading approaches and strategies. Therefore, you, like this market, should be a little bit non-standard in your thinking, flexible and be able to adapt to every situation in the market.

Despite the fact that, thanks to my book, you have gained a large amount of knowledge to understand cryptocurrency trading, do not forget that this "craft" cannot be mastered through books. Trading is not about theory, it's about practice. To yield a good result, read additional trading literature, but most importantly, make your first deals in parallel with the training. Start with a minimum amount. It will not bring you a large profit, but it will give you the necessary experience to move in the right direction.

Understanding the importance of practice, I included homework in my book. If you did the homework after each section of the book, you had to get rid of the fear of the "empty" price chart and now you know what to do with it.

Experience is important in trading like in many other areas. But what should you do if you are an absolute newbie in this field? If you are afraid of making deals, if you are not sure about your forecasts and you are afraid for your investment portfolio, then the next few paragraphs are for you. Yes, friends, there is always a way out. This way is called *demo account*.

A demo account serves as a pass for most newbies, giving them the right to start trading without spending real money. Some traders decide to open real transactions on the exchange after they reach a stable profit on a demo account. That's a winning strategy.

Many newbies rush straight into trading off the deep end. As soon as they get used to the interface of Tradingview platform and some kind of exchange, they open real accounts and try to trade. In most cases, the result of such attempts is not successful. Many lose interest in trading at this stage, are frustrated, and go to other areas of activity, telling everyone "cryptocurrency is a scam."

But how could it be otherwise, if yesterday this newcomer had no idea what technical analysis was, and today he is trying to convince himself that a triangle pattern appears on the chart? That's why I recommend all newbies pass a sort of "exam" on a demo account before embarking on trading on real accounts (especially during a falling and unpredictable market). A newcomer should achieve stable positive trading results on a demo account for at least one month (if we are talking about intraday or medium-term trading). For long-term strategies, it will take even more time to get prepared. I assure you that this time will not be wasted, because you can also test your trading strategy in real time during this period.

I will tell you my personal story. When my wife (a journalist by training) started to master trading, the comprehension of theory was far easier for her than pressing a buttons on the exchange. She had been creating forecasts on Tradingview platform for a long time but she did not dare to place her first order. I wanted to support her, but at the same time I understood that I shouldn't put pressure on her. Everything should take its course. Therefore, I recommended opening her first deal on a demo account. Trading on a virtual demo account helped her to get the necessary initial experience, make sure her predictions were correct and giver her confidence when she placed her first real order on a cryptocurrency exchange.

I am sure that an idea flashed through your mind: this example is not rational as her husband - a professional skilled trader - was next to this woman. Yes, I agree, it is much easier to go through all the stages of trading studies with a good teacher nearby. However, I, as a good teacher, never knocked my personal trading system into the head of my wife, because I know it is useless. My task was simple: to save her from making big mistakes and share my extensive experience with her. However, I did the same for you in my book. After reading it and hearing about my experience, you have to go through all the trading stages on your own, develop your understanding of the market, because you will build up or lose your capital, not mine.

At first, it may seem to you that everything is simple. But you know what? That's not how it works. Everything is much more difficult and easier at the same time. Here comes the drum roll: there is **no ready-made secret of success in trading**. What tough luck, friends: there are plenty of pitfalls in trading but no ready-made recipe for success :) But you can try to create your own recipe.

There is one art of a professional trader: to get the percentage in the black, increasing the positive expected value of your transactions. Only a sober, clear mind will lead a cryptocurrency trader to success. The ability to see pros where others see cons. The ability to earn wherever a trader is satisfied with the profit /

risk ratio. But never forget one financial rule: the **world of money does not tolerate blockheads**.

If you were happy that you grasped the basics of technical analysis and got prepared to trade with the help of charts only, then you are mistaken. Trading only with technical analysis is like running on one leg.

I by no means urge you not to look at the charts. At the same time, I ask you not to forget about the need to analyze the market depth, to study the psychology of the crowd and the psychology of big players. If, for example, you see the Triangle pattern on the price chart, be sure to answer the following questions before entering a trade: what the crowd wants now and what the big player wants. Continue to do technical analysis in combination with the answers to these questions.

If your coin shows a drawdown of 10%, 20% or 30%, should you be quick to sell it or not? Perhaps someone is trying to intimidate you? Maybe, the big players gain a foothold thanks to the alarmists like you? Try not to look at the market as if through a narrow window. Get up from your chair and look at the market from above. If the big players depressed the price so low and bought up 50% of coins in the market, then does it make sense for them to drop the price even lower by another 50%? I believe, no.

During technical analysis, obey the following rules in the same sequence:

- Identify significant levels and lines to get the zones, near which the price will "move" and where you, accordingly, will look for signals
- Look for candlestick patterns
- Choose only high-quality signals. Sometimes you need to wait for a confirmation candlestick in order to understand whether a signal is high-quality or not
- Follow the graphical patterns: look at the chart from different sides and be careful: maybe you have not noticed something, add indicators and oscillators, detect divergences
- Identify entry and exit points
- And only then place pending orders

Remember that there are three options for developments in the market:

- Buy
- Sell
- Do nothing

If you do not understand what you should do in particular situation (especially during a drawdown), then just wait. It's better not to earn money than to lose your coins for the pleasure of big players. Therefore, doing nothing is not always the worst option. It's better to do nothing than to make a lot of mistakes.

Therefore, before making a deal, think carefully and do not place an order if you are not sure of an entry point. If a signal that you received in the process of technical analysis is not qualitative (strong), do not open a position as it is better to make a smaller number of transactions with a lower risk than a lot of transactions, the major part of which will be unprofitable. If you notice that you missed a good entry point, do not enter; do not catch up with the train, which has already left.

Always work on your trading strategy, improve it, but do not apply it for each coin as an adamant axiom. Your trading strategy should have one clear and unchanging rule: you need to determine the entry and exit points before opening a position.

As for start-up capital for trading, its size does not matter much, because the main thing is what the market requires for successful work: not the amount of money with which you enter it, but the ability to constantly improve yourself in understanding the mechanisms of the market and the interests of its participants.

In a word, the cryptocurrency market now attracts most people because it is open to newbies and offers great prospects.

Even during a long drawdown, all professional traders know that sooner or later the downtrend will end, and only the smartest and the most dedicated cryptocurrency professionals will remain in the game at the time of the start of new uptrend. That is why the study of cryptocurrency trading is very useful. Do not give up, because **everyone has equal opportunities in this market**. Success depends on your personal efforts and your potential. If you are still waiting for miracles, I can tell you: there won't be any :)

Do the hard work necessary to be a step ahead!

Wish you a lot of profits and see you soon :)

GLOSSARY OF CRYPTOCURRENCY TERMS

Cryptocurrency is digital money created on certain algorithms using cryptography. The word "cryptos" means "secret" in Greek, hence the name of digital money. A cryptocurrency is difficult to counterfeit because of this security feature. It is also characterized by audibility, which means that cryptocurrency transactions are publicly available for verification. Cryptocurrency is decentralized (independent of any single computer). Cryptocurrency has a creator (a programmer wrote the code) but has no owner, who could take everything away from everyone, forcibly devalue or prohibit its use.

Satoshi is the smallest indivisible unit of Bitcoin. It is named after Satoshi Nakamoto, the creator of Bitcoin. One Bitcoin contains one hundred million Satoshis, so it is a one hundred millionth of a single Bitcoin (0.00000001 BTC).

Altcoin is alternative cryptocurrency. After Bitcoin gained popularity, new coins appeared in abundance. Most of them disappeared as quietly as emerged, but some have gained sort of popularity.

Mining is a process of using a computer, a farm, ASICs for mining cryptocurrency. In fact, a computer consumes electricity and uses its computing capacities to find the necessary code sequence, i.e., it solves math problems. Mining can be called a "printing press" as cryptocurrency can be exchanged for "fiat money" or goods.

Miner is a person engaged in cryptocurrency extraction using all possible means to perform the necessary computing operations. Personal computers, laptops and smartphones are suitable for this purpose (although smartphones are extremely exposed to risk of overheating and failure, so now it is ineffective). The profitability of cryptocurrency mining at home tends to be ineffective, so advanced miners have become farmers and mine cryptocurrency using specialized equipment - farms and ASICs.

ASIC is an application-specific integrated circuit. This means that ASIC can be used for a specific task or a narrow range of tasks. As applied to cryptocurrency mining, ASICs are customized to work with a set of algorithms, which increases their efficiency in comparison with personal computers, but only in a narrow area – cryptocurrency mining.

Farm is the equipment intended for cryptocurrency mining. Farm productivity varies depending on hardware and software optimization, but all farms are characterized with high power consumption and high heat dissipation, so they need to be cooled.

Cloud mining is a mechanism when an investor is offered to buy computing power for cryptocurrency mining. The process of mining takes place automatically, without your participation. It is popular because of the high cost of mining equipment and increase in complexity of the network.

PoS mining (proof of stake) is extraction of cryptocurrency via storing a certain amount of it in the wallet. For example, if you have certain amount of cryptocurrency coins stored in your wallet, you will receive additional coins for storage.

Masternode (proof of stake) is a technology that can be purchased from cryptocurrency developers to increase profitability of PoS mining.

Pool is a service presented by a website on the Internet that is simultaneously used by a large number of miners to mine cryptocurrency. A pool can be both specialized (its members mine the same cryptocurrency) or diversified (its members mine different types of cryptocurrency). The pool allows the participants not to worry about the storage of the cryptocurrency they have acquired, although there have been cases when pools deceived miners into parting with money. Therefore, old, popular pools considered to be reliable and honest are of particular value.

Network complexity is a parameter that reduces the likelihood of finding the right piece of a code at certain time intervals. At such a moment, the miners say "network complexity has increased." In other words, less Bitcoin will be mined tomorrow than yesterday, if the technical capacities do not change. That is why the technical capacities are constantly increasing and improving as equipment becomes obsolete within a few months.

Bitcoin address is a unique combination of uppercase and lowercase Latin letters and numbers of 34 characters or less. Most Bitcoin addresses consist of 34 or 33 characters, but may contain less than 30 characters. This is explained by the presence of zeros at the beginning of the address: if zeros are omitted, the "short" address remains. Each Bitcoin address is unique. It is written in blockchain and therefore the creation of two identical ones is impossible.

Bitcoin wallet is software or a website installed on a computer or a smartphone that allows storing keys and performing operations of sending, storing and receiving Bitcoin. In fact, a wallet does not store Bitcoin, it only contains keys for accessing some Bitcoin in the general network. However, the loss of a wallet leads to the loss of keys, which makes the Bitcoin linked to these keys inaccessible.

Transaction is transfer of currency from one wallet to another.

Pending is unfinished transaction in progress.

Fork is a cryptocurrency that appeared later, a partial analogue of its predecessor.

ICO is release of cryptocurrency on public exchange.

Tokens are cryptocurrency before the ICO release.

Crowdsale is the primary purchase of future cryptocurrency tokens prior to ICO.

Bulls are stock market players who buy cheap goods and sell them at the peak price. Thus, they speculate only for a rise.

Bears are traders who speculate for a fall, often deliberately knocking the price down to the lowest point.

Pump is intentional purchase of assets in huge quantities, aimed at short-term artificial price rise.

Dump is intentional sale of assets in huge quantities, aimed at short-term artificial price decline.

Money hold is restriction on use, deposit or withdrawal of funds on the exchange.

Order is a bid placed to buy or sell a certain amount of cryptocurrency.

Market depth is the quantity of the nearest cryptocurrency buy and sell orders.

Swing is short-term spikes in a small price range.

Peak is the highest price within a certain period of time, which is followed by decline.

Fiat is a broker slang word for any currency except for cryptocurrency.

ABOUT THE AUTHOR

Alan T. Norman is a proud, savvy, and ethical hacker from San Francisco City. After receiving a Bachelor's of Science at Stanford University. Alan now works for a mid-size Informational Technology Firm in the heart of SFC. He aspires to work for the United States government as a security hacker, but also loves teaching others about the future of technology. Alan firmly believes that the future will heavily rely computer "geeks" for both security and the successes of companies and future jobs alike. In his spare time, he loves to analyze and scrutinize everything about the game of basketball.

BONUS BOOK

Cryptocurrency Market Manipulations
and How I Found Satoshi Nakamoto

Link on the book: http://bit.ly/alans-bonus-book

You can scan QR code below to go by link. You'll need a Facebook account to get the book.

OTHER BOOKS BY THE AUTHOR

Mastering Bitcoin for Starters *(http://amzn.to/2AwSNy0)*

Cryptocurrency Investing Bible

(http://amzn.to/2zzB8IP)

Blockchain Technology Explained http://mybook.to/BlockchainExplained

Hacking: Computer Hacking Beginners Guide
(www.amazon.com/dp/B01N4FFHMW)

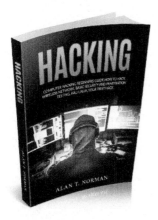

Hacking: How to Make Your Own Keylogger in C++ Programming
Language

HACKED: Kali Linux and Wireless Hacking Ultimate Guide
(https://www.amazon.com/dp/B0791WSRNZ)

One Last Thing...

DID YOU ENJOY THE BOOK?

IF SO, THEN LET ME KNOW BY LEAVING A REVIEW ON AMAZON! Reviews are the lifeblood of independent authors. I would appreciate even a few words and rating if that's all you have time for

IF YOU DID NOT LIKE THIS BOOK, THEN PLEASE TELL ME! Email me at alannormanit@gmail.com and let me know what you didn't like! Perhaps I can change it. In today's world a book doesn't have to be stagnant, it can improve with time and feedback from readers like you. You can impact this book, and I welcome your feedback. Help make this book better for everyone!